Mindfulness and Mental Health

Therapy, theory and science

Chris Mace

Routledge
Taylor & Francis Group

LONDON AND NEW YORK

First published 2008
by Routledge
27 Church Road, Hove, East Sussex BN3 2FA

Simultaneously published in the USA and Canada
by Routledge
270 Madison Avenue, New York, NY 10016

Reprinted 2008

Routledge is an imprint of the Taylor & Francis Group, an Informa business

Typeset in Times by Garfield Morgan, Swansea, West Glamorgan
Printed and bound in Great Britain by TJ International Ltd, Padstow,
Cornwall
Paperback cover design by Lisa Dynan

This publication has been produced with paper manufactured to strict
environmental standards and with pulp derived from sustainable forests.

British Library Cataloguing in Publication Data
A catalogue record for this book is available from the British Library

Library of Congress Cataloging-in-Publication Data
Mace, Chris, 1956–
  Mindfulness and mental health : therapy, theory, and science / Chris
Mace.
        p. ; cm.
  Includes bibliographical references and index.
  ISBN 978-1-58391-787-9 (hbk) – ISBN 978-1-58391-788-6 (pbk.)
  1. Mental health—Religious aspects—Buddhism. 2. Awareness. 3.
Meditation—Buddhism. I. Title.
  [DNLM: 1. Cognitive Therapy—methods. 2. Awareness. 3. Buddhism.
4. Meditation—psychology. 5. Religion and Psychology. WM 425.5.C6
M141m 2007]
  BQ4570.M4M33 2007
  294.3'37622–dc22

                                                        2007013929

ISBN: 978-1-58391-787-9 (hbk)
ISBN: 978-1-58391-788-6 (pbk)

Mindfulness and Mental Health

Being mindful can help people feel calmer and more fully alive. *Mindfulness and Mental Health* examines other effects it can also have and presents a significant new model of how mindful awareness may influence different forms of mental suffering.

The book assesses current understandings of what mindfulness is, what it leads to, and how and when it can help. It looks at the roots and significance of mindfulness in Buddhist psychology and at the strengths and limitations of recent scientific investigations. A survey of relationships between mindfulness practice and established forms of psychotherapy introduces evaluations of recent clinical work where mindfulness has been used with a wide range of psychological disorders. As well as considering current 'mindfulness-based' therapies, future directions for the development of new techniques, their selection, how they are used and implications for professional training are discussed. Finally, mindfulness's future contribution to positive mental health is examined with reference to vulnerability to illness, adaptation and the flourishing of hidden capabilities.

As a cogent summary of the field that addresses many key questions, *Mindfulness and Mental Health* is likely to help therapists from all professional backgrounds in getting to grips with developments that are becoming too significant to ignore.

Chris Mace is Consultant Psychotherapist to Coventry and Warwickshire NHS Partnership Trust and honorary Senior Lecturer in Psychotherapy at the University of Warwick. He is currently chair of the Royal College of Psychiatrists' Psychotherapy Faculty. His previous publications include the Routledge handbooks *The Art and Science of Assessment in Psychotherapy*; *Heart and Soul: The therapeutic face of philosophy*; and *Evidence in the Psychological Therapies*.

Contents

Preface

I had not realised before starting work on this book how much attention had influenced my thinking about mental illness and mental health. In the 1980s, I had been greatly intrigued by Pierre Janet's descriptions of attentional debility as a pathognomonic sign of hysteria. According to Janet, the (usually female) hysterical patient differed from others in an inability to talk and tap her fingers on command at the same time. As this apparently simple bedside test appeared never to have been evaluated, I spent months of painstaking work in developing a computerised testing tool that could quantify the degree of interference between concurrent tasks and identify which operations were most sensitive to interference. I had to learn rather more then than I do now about computer programming, but the outcome of the tests carried out on patients with hysterical symptoms was, to put it mildly, messy. These subjects found so many unanticipated ways of doing them badly, from failing to learn the required actions in their simplest form despite repeated rehearsals, to doing the exact opposite of whatever was requested with astonishing facility. The exercise provided an excellent introduction to some of the definitional difficulties to be faced in any attempt to operationalise attention, even if these were to be dwarfed by the effort of defining 'hysteria'.

At that time, any interest in 'attention' – as opposed to 'information processing' – was quite unfashionable. A few psychopathologists such as Meldman had already indicated how attention could be a very valuable key to understanding why some mental symptoms were so debilitating, and in producing relatively useful and apparently valid criteria for when one mental disorder became a different one (Meldman, 1970). Since then, almost all of my work has been in clinical psychotherapy, puzzling over rather different problems. One recurrent puzzle has been why one therapy works out well in practice when another, apparently similar in most important ways, unexpectedly does not. There is usually no lack of ways in which the failure of one therapy can be rationalised after the event if there is a wish to do so. However, after discussing, supervising and conducting many hundreds of psychotherapeutic interventions, I am persuaded there are critical aspects to the therapeutic process, often unrecognised, that are to do with attention within the treatment.

Another problem comes from relating what happens in practice to psychotherapeutic theory. In differing clinical situations, help has been forthcoming from the least expected quarters sufficiently often to keep me doubting that the apparent differences between schools and models of therapy are as real, necessary or helpful as is often claimed. The arrival of psychotherapeutic methods that claim to work by modifying attentional processes cuts across these boundaries, posing a challenge to favoured explanations on all sides. The possibility that these innovations might be transformative, not only for individuals but for how we think about what is therapeutic, has been an intriguing one.

The nature of mindful attention taps into a third sort of professional concern. An important strand of my work involves teaching, sometimes to reluctant students. Whether the context for this is teaching medical students about psychotherapy, or teaching psychotherapists about research, I continue to be amazed at people's ability, when faced with unfamiliar language, and misleading prior assumptions, to deny or to forget what they in fact already know. It seems to me that, with its overtly simple invitation to look inside and be aware of what is already there, mindfulness offers one kind of corrective to a trend that is otherwise insidious and growing.

An analogy here may help. There are still many, if rapidly dwindling, areas of Britain where, after dark, the stars of the night sky can be seen clearly. Whether or not it is felt as awesome, the view manages to be literally infinite, yet unique to the spot from which it is seen. Until the last century, the night sky has been fundamental to our sense of orientation, as well as a vital source of artistic, philosophical and scientific inspiration across all major cultures. Yet it can be effectively obliterated not only by doors and shutters, but by fixed lights intended to illuminate the ground just in front of us. This artificial light helps many mundane tasks to continue, but at the same time shuts out the view of the heavens that would otherwise have been there. It is unlikely to make sense to turn off street lights if they have always stood in the same place and their utility is obvious. But the analogy that it might be possible to see far further by being willing to see a little less holds good. There is also the possibility that what is then seen is also accessible to anyone, anywhere. A determination to turn away from the light in order to see something that is more subtle would also involve recollecting something that had been forgotten, rather than seeing only things whose apparent newness is that of a show manufactured for local consumption.

What follows is an investigation of what mindfulness means, is, and can and cannot do. Like other aspects of consciousness, it is formless, wordless and invisible, so the provisional findings offered here have to be written as an account of what people have done with mindfulness. It will be for you to take from these as you please, and to go on seeing what, if anything, mindfulness has to offer you. One comment may help with this process, against which this or any other offerings on the subject might be tested. Are you being invited to buy into a new lighting system that someone else will kindly switch on for you, so you can see ahead a little better? Or are obstructions being removed, however slightly, so you may look behind appearances and see everything that arises in a different light?

Chris Mace
October 2006

Acknowledgements

I have been grateful for conversations and exchanges with many people while preparing this book. They include: Alberto Albeniz, Jim Austin, Ruth Baer, Scott Bishop, Kirk Brown, Becca Crane, Larry Culliford, Petah Digby-Stewart, David Elias, Pam Erdman, Peter Fenwick, David Fontana, Paul Gilbert, Paul Grossman, Myra Hemmings, Jon Kabat-Zinn, Les Lancaster, Barry Magid, Susie van Marle, Dale Mathers, Stirling Moorey, Tony Parsons, Judith Soulsby, Nigel Wellings, Mark Williams and Polly Young-Eisendrath, None of them are at all responsible for its contents. I remain indebted to the six volunteers who assisted with the study summarised here in Chapter 2. I am also grateful for the stimulus of the many writers whose work is briefly quoted and reviewed here in line with 'fair dealing' conventions. Coleman Barks' reconstruction of Rumi's 'Guest House' is printed with his permission on behalf of Maypop Books; 'Wild Geese' from *Dream Work* by Mary Oliver (Copyright © 1986 by Mary Oliver) is used by permission of Grove/Atlantic, Inc. I thank a former employer, the South Warwickshire Primary Care Trust, and my clinical colleagues there, for granting and covering the study leave in which some essential research for the book was undertaken.

Since the book was commissioned, life has been more than usually tumultuous. I thank the publishers for their forbearance. It is dedicated to my (late) mother, Betty Mace. She contributed greatly to my own good health, as well as that of very many others.

Introduction

Mindfulness is a way of being aware. Mindful awareness is receptive and not exclusive. Sensations, thoughts, or feelings are simply experienced for what they are. To be mindfully aware means, strangely, there can be an absence of 'mind'. Even if thoughts are chattering away, they receive no more attention than anything else that has arisen. As people's ordinary, reactive ways of restricting their awareness diminish, a sense of the suchness of things emerges. At the same time, being mindful does not mean that the mind falls silent, or expands, or radiates universal love. These may happen, in awareness, but they are not the process itself.

The experience of mindfulness seems to come more easily to some people than others. It can be enhanced by practising exercises, ancient and new, to bring mindfulness about. However, these never carry a guarantee. Until relatively recently, when people strove to become more 'mindful', it would be for essentially spiritual purposes, as part of an interconnected system of practice and belief allied to a community or organisation. While the practice might often bring a subjective sense of equanimity and well-being, this was neither its primary purpose in such a context, nor would it be possible to attribute those subjective effects to one element of the system alone.

Currently, we find ourselves in an age saturated at the same time by instant communication, cultural fusion and religious intolerance. In contemporary lives, personal happiness has less to do with individual circumstances than most people assume. Yet, 'depression' is set to dominate the World Health Organisation's problem list from around 2020. Consider these developments together, and other trends make sense. In searching for new and potentially potent ways of both alleviating and preventing mental health problems, there is a receptivity to approaches that, crudely put, do not try to change the facts as much as the response to the facts. There is also an understandable wish to present this in terms that should not upset anybody's religious sensibilities.

The number of mindfulness-based interventions is continuing to multiply and their range of influence to expand. It may be too early to know if they are here to stay and, if so, in what format they will survive. However, they are already difficult for mental health professionals and their clients to ignore. What is more, they tend to engender a good deal of enthusiasm if people have first-hand experience of their considerable potential for stress relief, or if they have found their underlying philosophy appealing. This book comes as an orientation to what it seems realistic to expect mindfulness to have to offer mental health – whether this is conceived narrowly in terms of the management of mental disorders, or more broadly as realising otherwise latent potentials.

In surveying the contributions mindfulness can make, the book visits several distinct kinds of terrain. The principal ones include early Buddhist philosophy, brain and psychological science, and abnormal and 'positive' psychology, as well as therapeutics. Each terrain could be likened to a continent that can be characterised in terms of not only its geography but also its relationships and the human cultures it has supported and become indelibly associated with. On the first continent, religious communities have flourished, and an interest in the inner life has pervaded all forms of culture. On the second, an unshakeable confidence in the power of reason and the need to look out toward the rest of the natural world has brought domination of the environment and endless experiments in social engineering. The third and fourth are interlinked in that they identify themselves through a moral compass in which there is a strong sense of what is desirable and undesirable, right and wrong. Their mores are sufficiently different for each to claim a monopoly in the first, and that the other is a bastion of what is undesirable and wrong.

The fifth continent lies at the heart of the others. There may be least to show in terms of visible or intellectual achievement: its strengths are to do with the arts of meeting and influence. Such a continent arouses deep passions and distrust from outside itself. It is seen by others as the dark continent. Outsiders' fascination keeps it alive, while their fear prevents them from ever supporting it fully.

These contrasts bear no possible relationship to actual worlds, of course, but they can express some of the differences between the worlds of Oriental philosophy, science, normal and abnormal psychology, and psychotherapy. An expedition may be started anywhere along a route and a book of maps can be opened at will. While there is a planned route through the pages that follow, with later chapters referring back to earlier ones, it is likely to be heavy going for a complete newcomer to the subject. The first two chapters particularly might be skipped in a first reading, and then returned to later. Throughout, brief summaries are provided at the end of each chapter to assist strategic readers in their navigation.

Finally, I hope these tentative sketches will be the basis for future revisions. Interest in mindfulness is rapidly growing, particularly among mental health professionals, and it is often difficult to determine when new work has something important to contribute. Any offers to make me better aware of some of the work that will have inevitably been missed in a first book of this kind would be gratefully and kindly received.

c/o Department of Psychology
University of Warwick
Coventry CV4 7AL
UK

rstanding mindfulness:
⌐ igins

> There is no mental process concerned with knowing and under-standing, that is without mindfulness.
>
> Commentary on the *Satipatthana Sutta*,
> cited by Thera (1965: 194)

Defining mindfulness

Mindfulness means paying attention in a particular way: on purpose, in the present moment, and nonjudgmentally.

(Kabat-Zinn 1994: 4)

(a) Mindfulness reminds us of what we are supposed to be doing; (b) it sees things as they really are; and (c) it sees the true nature of all phenomena.

(Gunaratana 1992: 156)

In mindfulness, the meditator methodically faces the bare facts of his experience, seeing each event as though occurring for the first time.

(Goleman 1988: 20)

[Mindfulness is] keeping one's consciousness alive to the present reality.

(Hanh 1991: 11)

[Mindfulness is] awareness of present experience with acceptance.

(Germer 2005b: 7)

What is it to be mindful? It is to pay attention in a particular way. Is it possible to say what way that is? It is, and these quotations represent attempts by different authors to do so. Some write from the standpoint of Buddhism and some from that of psychology. There is an emphasis on awareness being alive to what is immediately presented to it, at the expense of other kinds of experience, and on this being accepted without judgement. Beyond these points, there can be subtle but significant differences between one conception of 'mindfulness' and the next, with different facets of mindfulness being given more emphasis and priority over others by different commentators.

So what quality might typify mindful awareness? In some definitions it is apparently directed, and focused by deliberate effort. (Jon Kabat-Zinn helpfully uses the word 'intentionality' in this context.) At the same time, it has been characterised by others as a broad, inclusive and receptive awareness, in contrast to the restriction of attention that results from concentration (e.g. Speeth 1982; Goleman 1988). Does mindfulness have a particular object? From the above definitions, it would seem not. Yet, awareness of internal processes such as breathing, body sensations, thoughts and feelings has been essential to the various methods of teaching it, along with a varying emphasis on mindfulness of external objects apparent through vision and hearing. Does mindful perception have a particular quality? The qualities of acceptance and non-judgement are prominent in most accounts, as the definitions cited confirm. Is there an emotional tone to mindfulness? To some, it is absolutely neutral, with an experience of equanimity being emphasised: to others (including Thich Nhat Hanh), it is closely interlinked with particular positive emotions of love or kindness.

For some commentators, a further key quality of mindfulness is its wordlessness: the immediacy of mindful awareness is a consequence of its being preconceptual and operating prior to experiences becoming labelled through thinking. This point is less than straightforward. As N. Thera has pointed out (1994: 80–1), there are several examples in the Buddhist instructional texts of the deliberate naming of experience being used as a means of becoming mindful of them. Indeed, these techniques have been copied in some contemporary therapists' methods for teaching their patients 'mindfulness skills' (cf. Chapter 3). Then there is the association of mindfulness with presentness: being mindful is to be alert to what is happening now to the exclusion of the past or the future. While this is seen as a key characteristic in many modern discussions, it has no real equivalent in the canonical Buddhist literature. Instead, the latter sometimes emphasises recollection as a key aspect of mindfulness.

Therefore one does not have to go very far or very deep to see that there is much scope for divergence between conceptions of mindfulness. They may be describing different things, in which case a corrective analysis is overdue. Or they may be separately failing to capture something that, like the elephant being felt in different places by six blind men, is simply bigger and more varied than any of them have allowed for. Gunaratana, who provides what is apparently the most complex (and, as will be seen, traditional) of the definitions above, argues that 'Mindfulness is extremely difficult to define in words – not because it is complex, but because it is too simple and open' (Gunaratana 1992: 154). He states that in any field, the most basic concepts are the hardest to pin down, precisely because they are the most fundamental, with everything else resting on them. This is why he has felt it better to try to say what mindfulness does rather than what it is, just as we might when trying to explain gravity. Unfortunately, this step does not necessarily resolve anything. Instead, it is likely to open up a related question of whether there is any characteristic understanding or knowledge to which mindfulness leads. The question is important and unavoidable. For instance, in North America, the terms 'insight meditation' and 'mindfulness meditation' can be used interchangeably, encouraging the presumption that mindfulness does affect understanding as well as perception. Whatever contemporary investigations may have to say about the contribution of mindfulness to insight, the connection is made in early Buddhist philosophy and is critical to an understanding of why the practice of mindfulness was valued. To understand mindfulness more fully, its Buddhist context needs to be acknowledged and, at least in its basics, understood.

Buddhist psychology

Buddhism has given rise to an extraordinarily complex body of teachings as it has diversified over 2500 years. Despite many disagreements over particulars, awareness remains central to all of them. The account that follows will draw primarily on the earliest Buddhist teachings. The works of this Theravadan tradition not only have a clearer linkage to the sayings and practice of Buddhism's founder, but also have been the most influential in modern adaptations of 'mindfulness'. The main purpose in looking at the Buddhist context of mindfulness here will be to examine what it was expected to achieve. This is useful in making sense of its methods (as well as the lengths people were prepared to go to in developing it). It is also an important preparation for evaluating the uses to which it is being put now.

Any attempt to discuss this literature needs to be accompanied by a strong health warning concerning the problems of translation. The divisions between units of meaning encoded in the ancient languages Pali or Sanskrit rarely coincide with those found in modern languages. Translation is far more difficult as a result. This is compounded by grammatical incompatibilities in which verbs convey radically different modes of action from their modern counterparts. The need for caution is well illustrated by the history of 'mindfulness'. 'Mindfulness' was introduced a century ago by the translator Rhys David when working on Pali texts for the Buddhist Text Society. He used it to translate the Pali term *sati*, for which common alternative translations are 'awareness' or 'bare attention'. *Sati* itself has broader connotations, however. Some of these, such as the capacity to tidy the mind, are generally incorporated in 'mindfulness'. However, as might be expected from contemporary writers' stress on the 'present', the subsidiary meaning of *sati* as recollection of the past is usually not subsumed under 'mindfulness'. At the same time, other Pali terms, such as *appamada*, meaning 'ever present watchfulness or heedfulness in avoiding ill or doing good' (Thera 1974: 180) or 'non-negligence or absence of madness' (Gunaratana 1992: 158), can also be translated as 'mindfulness' in modern texts. It is, therefore, hard to claim complete authenticity or fidelity to the early texts on behalf of modern uses of 'mindfulness'. (In the remainder of this book, the term will be used in a way that is broadly equivalent to *sati* as 'bare attention', as many of the writers who have thought about mindfulness in clinical settings use it in this way.)

Overall, Buddhist theory has the character of an elaborate and systematic psychology rather than a theology or cosmology. Unlike Western psychologies, its concepts are always intended to support practical teaching, never losing a concern with attainment of liberation from various states of spiritual captivity. It is generally available in two formats. In one, the collections of *sutras* (Sanskrit) or *suttas* (Pali), ideas are presented within reports of talks given by the Buddha or a disciple that had his approval. They may be elaborated in dialogue with the monks who are invariably present, their practical importance being underlined by parables and injunctions to act in particular ways. In the other format, that of the systematic psychology known as the *Abhidhamma*, ideas are systematised using a common vocabulary, and the relations between them coded. The result is a huge reference compendium that also provides a map of the abstract relations underlying the different segments of the system. There are therefore important differences in content and style, with the *Abhidhamma* also probably post-dating the Theravadan *sutta* collections by at least two centuries.

Superficially, there are similarities with Greek writing of the time. The Buddha's contemporary, Socrates, also wrote nothing himself, but it is probable his ideas and teaching style are captured in the earliest of Plato's dialogues, in which Socrates appears as a character. However, unlike Buddha (and Plato himself), Socrates probably had no theoretical ideas that he felt he needed to impart in order to assist his students' personal growth (cf. Mace 1999b). When, in the hands of Aristotle, Greek philosophy does become more systematic, it is after much additional theorising. The *suttas* of the Buddhist canon are always unlike Socratic dialogues in being more clearly didactic and intended for rote learning. While it is relatively easy to trace at what point other minds have contributed to the systematisation of early Greek philosophy, an insistence on attributing all the subsequent ramifications of Buddhist psychology to the Buddha himself has made it extremely hard to attribute ideas to other protagonists in ordinary historical terms.

It is not necessary to examine the treatises providing exhaustive accounts of meditative practice to understand the core of Buddhist psychology. Manuals such as the *Visuddhimagga* (Buddhaghosa 1999) characteristically discern many potential levels and goals encountered in meditative practice, but do not necessarily explain why the progressions take the form that they do. For this, it is important to appreciate the most basic tenets of Buddhism and the Buddhist view of the mind.

The essence of Buddhist teaching, accepted by all schools whatever their other doctrinal disagreements, is expressed in the Four Noble Truths. These are that life brings suffering, that there are causes of this suffering, that suffering can end, and that there is a path by which it may be ended. It is in the elaboration of the last truth, in descriptions of how liberation might be attained, that mindfulness comes to the fore. The method of attaining liberation is set out in eight linked stages within the Noble Eightfold Path. These concern the attainment of morality (*sila*), concentration (*samadhi*) and wisdom (*panna*). Among the eight, the three factors that make for concentration are 'right effort', 'right awareness' and 'right concentration'. Mindfulness is an essential ingredient of 'right awareness' (often translated as 'right mindfulness') and, as such, the foundation of the mental discipline necessary to achieve concentration and, subseqently, the 'right understanding' and 'right thought' that make up wisdom.

To appreciate how the Noble Eightfold Path leads to liberation, the ontology that underpins it must also be understood. In Buddhist thought, being has three essential characteristics, usually translated as unsatisfactoriness or suffering (*dukka*), transcience (*anicca*) and absence of self (*anatta*). These qualities are interdependent, such that appreciation of the pervasiveness of one of them enhances appreciation of the others. In moving to the phenomenal world, the Buddha referred to five distinct types of aggregates that comprise our experience of the world and ourselves, namely, material form (*rupa*), feeling (*vedana*), perception (*sanna*), mental proliferations (*sankhara*) and consciousness (*vinaya*).

In accounting for the partiality of perception and its relationship to other functions such as thinking, Buddhist psychology intimately supports Buddhist practice. There is a series of stages by which, through the five aggregates, events give rise to knowing. Within early Buddhist literature, principal teachings have been presented for general consumption in the *suttas* as well as systematically in the *Abbidhamma*. The former are usually far more accessible, and can be turned to here to illustrate the key ideas.

The honeyball *sutta*

In the so-called honeyball *sutta* (a honeyball is a kind of sweet cake) (No. 18 of the *Majjhima Nikaya* or 'middle-length' discourses (Nanamoli and Bodhi 1995)), the Buddha is sitting in contemplation when a man approaches him aggressively and asks him what he proclaims. He is told the Buddha proclaims that one does not quarrel with anyone else, nor with the world's gods or rulers, because perceptions no longer sustain the man who achieves detachment from sensual pleasure. Such a man is free from confusion, worry, or any kind of craving. His questioner frowns, says nothing and departs. The Buddha goes to his disciples and tells them about his encounter. They ask him how it could be that perceptions no longer sustain the man who lives free from sensual pleasure, confusion, worry and craving. The Buddha replies they should look to the source of the perceptions and ideas that are tinged by 'mental proliferations'. If one no longer finds anything to delight in or cling to there, then all tendencies to craving, aversion, illusion, doubt and other unwholesome states of mind will end completely. Once he has said this, the Buddha leaves.

The monks realise his answer was incomplete and berate themselves for not having pressed the Buddha to explain more fully how this comes about. They go to a saintly man whom the Buddha had entrusted to provide reliable explanations and ask him to help them. The man is astonished at the opportunity the monks have passed up to question the source himself, but eventually he agrees to try to satisfy them. He explains that when forms are present to the eye, eye consciousness arises. When form, eye and eye consciousness meet, contact follows. From contact comes feeling. From feeling, perception. From perception, ideas. Through thinking, ideas lead to mental proliferation. Then he utters a crucial sentence: 'With what one has mentally proliferated as the source, perceptions and notions tinged by mental proliferation beset a man with respect to past, future, and present forms cognizable through the eye' (Nanamoli and Bodhi 1995: 203). This same circular sequence is then applied in turn to the ear and sounds, the nose and odours, the tongue and flavours, the body and physical sensations, and the mind and mental objects. Each time, the manifestations of contact, feeling, perception and thinking are acknowledged in turn. Each time, the consequent tainting of perceptions and ideas by mental proliferation is mentioned (even if these proliferations are not manifest in themselves). The saintly man goes on to explain that, when there is no eye, no form and no eye consciousness, there can be no manifestation of contact. If there is no manifestation of contact, there can be no manifestation of feeling. If there is no manifestation of feeling, there can be no manifestation of perception. If there is no manifestation of perception, there can be no manifestation of thinking. If there is no manifestation of thinking, there is no manifestation of being that is beset by perceptions and notions tinged by mental proliferation.

He says this is his understanding of how, if one no longer finds anything to delight in or cling to, then all tendencies to craving, aversion, illusion, doubt and other unwholesome states of mind will end completely. The monks are relieved at what they hear. When they tell the Buddha of this explanation, they are told he would have explained it in the same way, enjoining them to remember what they have now heard. When one monk likens its reviving effect to coming upon a honeyball after being weakened by hunger and exhaustion, the Buddha suggests that they might remember the discourse in future as the honeyball discourse.

Although it has been truncated here, the *sutta* is full of the rhythm and repetition that was calculated to aid its memorisation. Its simple, five-step exposition of the aggregates is inseparable from the explanation of the benefits of disaggregating them by deliberate mental purification.

In the more systematic writings of the *Abbidhamma*, a more differentiated account of the same mental levels is presented. Although 17 stages of perception are described there (see Lancaster 2004: 110, for a helpful diagrammatic summary), these reduce in essentials to the stages of the honeyball sutta. In staying with this simple model, in which cognition is related to the five broad aggregates of form, feeling, perception, mental proliferations and consciousness, some important qualifications must be added. One is that none of these translations are truly equivalent to the original terms. Two instances of how this can be practically significant will be mentioned.

The term used for 'feeling' (*vedana*) applies across physical and mental feeling, referring only to a fundamental movement toward or away from any object that is independent of its recognition. Feeling therefore always has one of only three characteristics (attraction, repulsion or neutrality). And in the practical disciplines that are intended to end the cycle of mental formation outlined in the *sutta*, value will be placed on meeting each with the same equanimity when they are encountered. Despite this, influential proponents of American Buddhism have interpreted 'feeling' here in a much more emotive way, using references to *vedana* in the *suttas* as an invitation to work through emotions of grief, sorrow and anger as part of a process of 'healing the heart' (cf. Kornfield 1993).

Conversely, *vedana*, like mental proliferation (*sankhara*), can sometimes, therefore, be translated by the term 'reaction'. However, the mental reactions of *sankhara* are balanced by the active part this tier of 'mental formation' plays in determining experience, making its translation by (mental) 'formation' or 'disposition' preferable to the term 'reaction'. *Sankhara* refers not only to elaborative thoughts and memories that are immediately present to awareness, but also to habits of mind that, in becoming established and deepened through repetition, could be described as unconscious. Consciousness (*vinaya*) is subject itself to aggregation (and therefore conditioning and limitation) but has a unique ontological status in that it ultimately subsumes the other four aggregates.

The prime characteristic that all these aggregates share is that they are conditioned, being known because of this as the 'five aggregates of clinging'. In being conditioned, they contribute to suffering (*dukka*). There is an important equation of the whole concept of suffering beyond what is overtly painful, to what is limited. Human experience is only possible with the participation of all five kinds of aggregate. Their interplay usually serves both to restrict current experience and to condition experiences in the future.

The exposition of the five aggregates in the honeyball *sutta* depended upon the Buddhist concept of the six senses. In addition to the five senses of touch, smell, taste, sight and hearing, the mind is regarded as a sixth sense organ. Although the repetitious references to each sensory system in turn can seem redundant, recognition of the independence of the systems ensures that separate attention is given to each kind of sensation, and also to the mind. The objects of the mind are mental contents such as thoughts. Experiences originating with the mind are as prone to conditioning as those arising through any other sense organ. Conditioning of the mind fosters the illusory appearance of permanence and self on which subjective psychological life is normally based, but which is antithetical to the Buddhist conception of reality as impermanent (*anicca*) and not organised around selves (*anatta*).

Several features of this Buddhist view of perception are at odds with Western assumptions. There will be no sensing 'I' to which all perceptual pathways ultimately lead. Instead, the process of seeing is distinct from that of hearing, each sense modality being bound up with its own form of consciousness. Perception is not some linear process that tracks from some objective external entity to some stable, experiencing ego. Rather, the way elementary forms are linked to one another in the course of cognition depends on the mental formations through which they are filtered. It follows that perception that is not tainted, even prior to the conscious registration of sensations, is virtually impossible, as distortions render the experience partial at each stage. The Western dichotomy between 'active' and 'passive' mental processes is misleading here, as perception is indissolubly active and passive. The whole system invites comparison with the most thorough account of cognition to be found in Western philosophy, that of Immanuel Kant (Kant 2003). Kant had to invoke a priori mental structures to account for the apparent unity of perception. The Buddhist account maintains that such apparent unity is imposed rather than necessary, while the quality of perceptions will differ from one experiencer to another according to the *shankaras* or mental formations that uniquely condition their experience.

The foundations of mindfulness

Mindfulness was a prerequisite for the liberation sketched in the fourth Noble Truth, its perfection being a key component of the method the Buddha discovered and urged his disciples to follow. The three kinds of step within the Noble Eightfold Path were mentioned earlier. One set is in the form of moral preparations (right living, right action and right speech). Another set involves an apprehension of the world as it is (right view and right intention). The remaining set is distinct from the actions of the first or the understandings of the second, being particular forms of mental discipline (right effort, right concentration and right mindfulness). It is often taught that this set represents the means by which the moral preparations making up the first set come to be realised as the wisdom of right view and right intention. This teaching places the attainment of mindfulness in a pivotal position in the attainment of liberation. Along with the proper exercise of concentration and effort, right mindfulness would bring about the dissolution of the aggregates that is necessary for cognition to lose its fetters and for liberation to follow.

While influential, this account of progression from actions through mental purification to wisdom is not the only possible one. Rupert Gethin points out that the traditional enumeration of the eight steps does not follow this sequence and that some attempt to understand the world in terms of suffering is likely to need to precede striving for liberation, rather than the other way around (Gethin 1995: 84). Gethin argues against any sequential conception, suggesting that the Noble Eightfold Path requires concurrent progress on all fronts, and that complete success is as likely to be the product of liberation as its means.

The practical importance of 'mindfulness' is certainly underscored in the teachings that set out how it should be attained. These are known as the four foundations (or establishings) of mindfulness. The *sutta* expounding them begins with the Buddha's declaration, 'There is, monks, this one way to the purification of beings, for the overcoming of sorrow and distress, for the disappearance of pain and sadness, for the gaining of the right path, for the realisation of Nibbana: that is to say the four foundations of mindfulness' (Walshe 1995: 335).

This has probably guaranteed that this *sutta* (the 'greater discourse on the foundations of mindfulness' or *Mahasatipatthana Sutta*) has been exceptionally popular, one translator, Maurice Walshe, observing, 'this is generally regarded as the most important sutta in the entire Pali canon' (Walshe 1995: 588). It provides a good vehicle for investigating how the practice of mindfulness was taught in early Buddhism. Like the honeyball *sutta*, the *Mahasatipatthana Sutta* was very practical in its intent and design. The translation of '*patthana*' as 'foundations' may suggest a theoretical work; as the alternative rendering of 'establishings' suggests (VRI 1996), its subject is how the meditator can found or establish mindfulness within himself or herself.

The four foundations the *Mahasatipatthana Sutta* covers are contemplation (*anupassana*) of the body, contemplation of feelings, contemplation of the mind, and contemplation of mind objects. Of these four domains, the first and the last receive far more attention in the *sutta* than the other two. Exercises to develop contemplation of the body are described in a series of six sections: 1. on breathing; 2. on postures; 3. on clear comprehension; 4. on the repulsiveness of the body; 5. on the material elements; 6. nine graveyard contemplations. These are followed by short sections on the contemplation of feelings (*vedana*) and contemplation of mind (*citta*). The final section on contemplation of mental objects (*dhamma*) provides instruction on contemplating five key doctrines of Buddhist teaching: 1. the five hindrances; 2. the five aggregates of clinging; 3. the six internal and external sense bases; 4. the seven factors of enlightenment; 5. the Four Noble Truths.

The *sutta* concludes with a promise that whoever practises these four foundations of mindfulness will achieve either 'highest knowledge' (*anna*) here and now, or, if there is still the slightest clinging, at least the state of non-return. (The former is equivalent to full liberation. The state of non-return means there would be no more earthly reincarnations before a future liberation.)

What kind of exercises are contained in these passages? The very first item under contemplation of the body, commonly translated as 'mindfulness of breathing', does contain clear instructions for maintaining attention on the passage of the breath in a seated posture. The first step is to breathe in and breathe out 'with awareness'. The next step is to know that when a breath is long, it is long, and when it is short, it is short. The next is for the meditator to train himself to feel the whole body as he breathes in and out. This, it is said, leads to calming of the body and the breath. An analogy is introduced at this point between the 'knowing' that is required of variation in the breath and the knowing that a wood turner has when making a long turn or a short turn. This applies also to the way the whole body is known. A new idea is introduced, that the meditator practise contemplation of the body 'internally, or externally, or both internally and externally'. This is followed by an exhortation to contemplate origination factors in the body, or dissolution factors, or both. In this way, the awareness, 'this is body', is established, through knowledge and awareness.

This reference to contemplating things 'internally, or externally, or both internally and externally' is quite puzzling. It is far from incidental, as it is repeated many times throughout the *sutta*, whenever a new practice is recommended. Modern teachers say relatively little about these phrases, suggesting that external contemplation involves awareness of the breathing of others while internal contemplation is awareness of the breathing of oneself (e.g. Silananda 2002: 24–5). However they might be interpreted, this aspect of this and all the other exercises in the *sutta* does not appear to be crucial, as it is omitted in alternative accounts such as the *sutta* on mindfulness of breathing (Nanamoli and Bodhi 1995: 941–8); or the *sutta* on the mindfulness of the body (949–58) within the same collection.

Despite the reverence in which the *Mahasatipatthana Sutta* is held, there have been significant variations between actual practices, even in monastic traditions, and the guidance in this *sutta*. Considerable emphasis on anchoring practice in awareness of the body, in terms of attention to the breath and to the body itself in the course of meditation, contrasts with the neglect of the later 'contemplations' about the body. As the founder of an international school of vipassana meditation comments, regarding all of the contemplations on repulsiveness, the body and the graveyard contemplations: 'This is just a beginning for those not in a position to observe reality inside. Impurity keeps overpowering them. Once they can think properly, they are fit to practice, either with respiration or directly with sensations' (Goenka 1988: 48).

However, the *sutta* reiterates the point of each contemplation in its own way: 'Truly, this body of mine too is of the same nature, it will become like that and will not escape from it.' Thus, at the beginning and the end of this long section, '[the meditator] dwells contemplating origination-factors in the body, or he dwells contemplating dissolution-factors in the body, or he dwells contemplating both origination- and dissolution-factors in the body. Or his mindfulness that "there is a body" is established in him to the extent necessary for knowledge and mindfulness. Independent he dwells, clinging to nothing in the world' (Thera 1965: 118). As the appreciation of constant origination and dissolution, moment by moment, is usually regarded as an advanced attainment (being a direct insight into impermanence), these 'contemplations' are likely to have an important primary function in the cultivation of mindfulness.

After the whole section on 'contemplation of the body', the *sutta* on the foundations of mindfulness proceeds to the three remaining sections. Of these, the last section on 'contemplation of mind-objects' is particularly extensive, moving through a range of teachings that outline the landscape the meditator faces. Most of these, including the five aggregates, the six sense spheres, the Four Noble Truths (incorporating the Noble Eightfold Path) have been mentioned already. The remaining two, which have not been mentioned, complement one other. They are the five hindrances and the seven enlightenment factors. The five hindrances (of desire, ill-will, drowsiness, agitation and doubt) are factors that, from the outset, stand in the way of attempts to establish mindful awareness. The seven factors of enlightenment (mindfulness, investigation of reality, energy, rapture, tranquillity, concentration and equanimity) are a longer list of the positive mental qualities that lead to liberation through insight. Mindfulness has a key position among them. Apart from being necessary for any of the others to develop, mindfulness is also seen as mediating between the three active factors (investigation, energy and rapture) and the three passive ones (concentration, tranquillity and equanimity). Its pre-eminent role is in maintaing a delicate and auspicious balance between the active and passive factors so that an optimal level of activity is maintained (Thera 1994: 89).

The various exercises appear to pose a fundamentally similar challenge: the objects in question need to be apprehended for what they are, as distinct experiences that arise and dissolve, impersonally and without attachment. This applies to the various aspects of the body, sensations, and mental states discussed through the *sutta*'s first three sections. Its final section, on mental objects, includes both negative contents (e.g. the five hindrances) as well as positive ones (e.g. the enlightenment factors). Because these are seen as intrinsically destructive or promotive of progress to insight and liberation, an initial phase in which they are discerned in a similar way to objects in earlier sections gives way to one in which active attention is given to the circumstances in which they have arisen. In this way, the hindrances are expected to loosen their hold, while the enlightenment factors are strengthened as they are experienced.

At its conclusion, after outlining the Four Noble Truths, the 'mental objects' section has a very similar coda to its predecessors:

> Or his mindfulness that 'there are mind-objects' is established in him to the extent necessary for knowledge and mindfulness. Independent he dwells, clinging to nothing in the world. Thus indeed, monks, a monk dwells practising mind-object contemplation on the mind-objects of the four Noble Truths.
>
> (Thera 1965: 125)

On the face of it, this is an injunction to strengthen the capacity to practise bare attention by resisting the subtle attraction of what are ordinarily the most essential teachings, in order to purify awareness until there is a direct, non-conceptual insight into reality. However, in broadly compatible ways, Nyanaponika Thera (1994) and Amadeo Sole-Leris (1992) both suggest that this task alters when the mental object is a fundamental doctrine about reality. With the cosmology of the five aggregates, and the spiritual message of the Four Noble Truths, the task becomes one of relating every other experience directly to those frameworks. Accordingly, each experience needs to be categorised in terms of its aggregate, so that the meditator develops an instinctive facility with the basic divisions of reality. Each reaction or action would be experienced in the light of the Four Noble Truths as any remaining attachment to it is loosened and a continuing, subliminal appreciation of the universality *of dukka, anicca* and *anatta* is confirmed. The result is the direct understanding with direct awareness the *sutta* speaks of.

The *sutta* ends, in effect, with a return to its beginning. It proclaims that it does not matter how long, or how short, a time the meditator takes. If the four foundations are developed as has been described (so that the student is independent, no longer clinging to any of the things that have been contemplated), final knowledge is attained, 'here and now'. If, instead, there is a trace of clinging left, the student's fate will be to become a non-returner.

The *sutta* is compact yet comprehensive. It does not exhaust the four foundations of mindfulness (there are more elaborate methods for achieving mindfulness of the body, for instance, requiring separate attention to all of its 39 constituents in Buddhist anatomy), but it provides both instruction and explanation. As with any pivotal text, there are many passages that have been subjected to minute examination and dispute. Some have already been indicated and there is little need to go further into the others here. However, one topic that is touched on in the *sutta* remains critical to an understanding of what mindfulness is and what it is not. This is the relationship of mindfulness to clear comprehension.

Mindfulness and clear comprehension

We have noted already how 'mindfulness' can have connotations of recollection, in the sense of self-awareness as well as recall of past events. While the latter is something that is likely to accompany increasing immediacy of awareness, awareness of an entire situation or gestalt classically shades into what is termed 'clear comprehension'. This is commonly found alongside mindfulness. Indeed, in the *sutta* on the foundations of mindfulness, 'mindfulness' is often being used to translate a compound word (*sati-sampajanna*) that (as in the joint references to knowledge and mindfulness in the translated *Mahasatipatthana Sutta*) refers to both at the same time. Nyanaponika Thera makes the distinction:

> Mindfulness is mostly linked with clear comprehension of the right purpose or suitability of an action, and other considerations. Thus again it is not viewed in itself. But to tap the actual and potential power of mindfulness it is necessary to

understand and deliberately cultivate it in its basic, unalloyed form, which we shall call bare attention. By bare attention we understand the clear and single-minded awareness of what actually happens to us and in us, at the successive moments of perception. It is called 'bare' because it attends to the bare facts of a perception without reacting to them by deed, speech or mental comment.

(Thera 1994: 72–3)

In its turn, 'clear comprehension' has four different referents, that is, comprehension of purpose; of appropriateness; of maintaining meditation; and of reality. This is clear from the *sutta*'s second section's treatment of 'contemplation of the body'. A subsection of it deals specifically with 'clear comprehension of the body'. There, over and above the use of the body as an object for bare attention, deliberate attention is paid to body postures and movements and also to the routine acts of everyday living. Sole-Leris comments:

In addition to broadening the scope for mindfulness, this exercise introduces a further element, described as 'clear comprehension'. This is the complement, at the intellectual level, of the mindful observation at the perceptual level. When meditation is carried out as an exclusive occupation in a motionless posture, whether seated, standing or lying down, it is, in fact, possible to exercise pure perceptual mindfulness. This is also possible – to all practical purposes – in the course of a period of formal walking meditation. But this is no longer the case when more complex activities are concerned involving . . . elements of intention, judgment, decision making, etc. By devoting to these mental components the same kind of deliberate attention as was paid to the bare sense data in the exercises just described, a clear comprehension is developed of the purpose of every action, of the best way of achieving that purpose . . . and of the exact nature of each act.

(Sole-Leris 1992: 87)

Elsewhere, it seems the 'clear comprehension' of reality is inseparable from bare attention. The original *sutta* refers repeatedly to '*sati-sampajanna*', while all four major translations of the *sutta* into English acknowledge the growth of understanding alongside awareness.

An untitled *sutta* in a related collection is even clearer about the interdependence of these capacities. In the 'connected discourses on the establishment of mindfulness', the Buddha declares: 'Bhikkhus [monks], a bhikkhu should dwell mindful and clearly comprehending: this is our instruction to you' (Bohdi 2000: 1628). This brief untitled *sutta* then leads to a summary of the four foundations of mindfulness (contemplating the body in the body, feelings in feelings, mind in mind, and (mental) phenomena in phenomena as before) followed by instructions on how and when clear comprehension is exercised. These dictate that a monk should act with clear comprehension when walking forward and back; when looking ahead and to the side; when stretching the limbs out and drawing them in; when wearing clothes and carrying his coat and bowl; when eating, drinking, chewing or tasting food; when at the toilet; when standing or sitting; when falling asleep or waking up; and when speaking or remaining silent. It ends with a reminder of the importance of clear comprehension as well as mindfulness (Bohdi 2000: 1628).

There may seem little point in driving home what can appear to be a somewhat scholastic distinction, but it is pertinent to two major themes of this book. One, to be taken up in Chapter 6, concerns the personal rewards of mindfulness practice. Although the *sutta* links liberation to mindfulness, the implication of additional practices such as clear comprehension suggests that mindfulness may not be sufficient on its own for such attainment. The second concerns the importance of isolating and defining mindfulness with precision, so that it might be investigated by the kind of scientific procedures that are discussed in the following chapter.

The ambiguity of mindfulness

This close interrelationship between mindfulness and clear comprehension goes some way to explaining the ambiguities of mindfulness noted at the start of this chapter. To understand some of the other associations, it may be practically important to recognise that, beyond the practices making up the 'foundations of mindfulness', other techniques are very commonly learned at the same time by students of Theravadan Buddhism. These include exercises designed to promote the *Brahmaviharas* or 'perfections', which develop higher, social feelings such as loving kindness, compassion and joy on others' behalf. When practised together, the *Brahmaviharas* are recognised to strengthen the capacity for bare attention, and vice versa.

As well as helping to explain the high valuation placed on mindfulness in Buddhist psychology, awareness of this background is useful in understanding how slightly different nuances become attached to the concept by different commentators and practitioners. Two recent examples of how teachers have made sense of the breadth of mindfulness by using traditional teachings can illustrate this.

Morgan and Morgan (2005: 76) draw on the interrelationship between the seven factors of enlightenment and learning mindfulness in practice. There is a well-respected tradition of learning mindfulness by deliberate cultivation of the qualities of investigation, energy, rapture, concentration, tranquillity and equanimity. (In fact, this strategy is at the core of the next most commonly used instructional *sutta* on mindfulness, the *Anapanasati Sutta* (Nanamoli 1964)). 'Mindfulness' can take on more or less of any of these factors because of their close association – without it being any less mindful. In a method that is reminiscent of teachers who use the *Anapanasati Sutta* directly (e.g. Rosenberg 1998), Morgan and Morgan turn this to practical use by encouraging their students to cultivate actively each of these qualities in order to deepen their attention.

An intriguing bid to harmonise different conceptions of mindfulness – and to argue for one in which underlying motivation and the transpersonal affects of the 'perfections' are emphasised – comes from Shauna Shapiro and colleagues (2006). In referring to Kabat-Zinn's widely cited definition of mindfulness in terms of deliberation, attention and non-judgement, they propose that differences in the quality of mindfulness can be understood in terms of three axes, labelled 'intention', 'attention' and 'attitude'. Each contributes to mindfulness, but the result as it is experienced by an individual, they suggest, depends upon the nature of the intention, attention and attitude. For this purpose, 'attention' refers to paying attention, and how far this is continuous, selective, and precursive; 'attitude' refers to how attention is paid. This can refer to qualities such as equanimity, curiosity or acceptance that inform the paying of attention. For Shapiro, who sees positive emotions such as compassion and loving kindness to be integral to mindfulness (she talks of 'heart-mindfulness'; cf. Chapter 5), attitudes of warmth and friendliness are inseparable from it. 'Intention' refers to the motivation leading to mindful practice and why it is undertaken. This understanding of intention is therefore different from either the sense of being deliberate in the way attention is paid, or from the Buddhist concept of 'right intention', which, in embracing qualities such as desirelessness, friendliness or compassion, is actually closer to what Shapiro calls 'attitude'. Once this is understood, it appears that the aspects of intention, attention and attitude start to correspond to the traditional subdivisions of morality, meditation and wisdom within the Noble Eightfold Path that were discussed earlier.

In this discussion of the 'origins' of mindfulness, it seemed appropriate to rely heavily on the early Buddhist texts from the Pali canon. This is not to imply that traditions that today continue to base themselves on these works enjoy a practical monopoly on mindful awareness. While other traditions have subsequently diverged considerably in their philosophies, they remain consistent with the basic ontology outlined here. Mindfulness is also key to other traditions' day-to-day practices, even if this may not be stressed in their literature. The translator Maurice Walshe observes: 'Among the Mahayans schools of the Far East, it is chiefly the Chinese Ch'an and Japanese Zen that are the closest to the spirit of Satipatthana' (Walshe 1995: 588). Although they differ in their aims, theory and methods, Walshe maintains that the links between Ch'an, Zen and Satipatthana are close and strong, even if they are rarely noticed. In support of this contention, he cites three common factors: 'the direct confrontation with actuality (including one's mind), the transcending of conceptual thought by direct observation and introspection; [and] the emphasis on the Here and Now' (Walshe 1995: 589).

The neuroscientist James Austin also comments on the closeness of Zen and vipassana, as they adopt similar methods for developing a 'nonreactive, bare awareness open to anything', where informal practice between sessions is just as important as formal sittings. Austin's comments here are also helpful in starting to move beyond origins to other aspects of mindfulness:

> Up to now, we have been describing how mindfulness meditation begins. But from here on it will evolve. Rarely does this point receive the emphasis it deserves. As it evolves, it proceeds in both external and internal dimensions along lines that are increasingly intuitive. So, on some brief occasions, paying bare

attention will turn into an outflowing: a totally appreciative, sacramental approach to the wondrous commonplace events of the present moment. At other times, bare attention turns inward. Now, its functions expand to include introspection and self-analysis. Personal matters rise into it spontaneously to become grist for the mill of intuition. Indeed, it then resembles psychoanalysis in the way it observes the topics it submits to intensive introspection.

(Austin 1998: 127)

Attentive readers will notice how Austin here felicitously resolves the issue of 'internal' and 'external' contemplation in terms of the perceived flow of attention. He also brings us to the next two arenas of the present survey: science and psychotherapy.

Conclusions

Contemporary definitions of mindfulness recognise an immediate and receptive awareness, shorn of reactions and judgement. Early Buddhist literature identifies a form of awareness, prior to the elaboration of experience through habitual reactions, which is known as 'bare attention' as well as 'mindfulness'. Mindfulness differs from the highly conditioned states of everyday awareness, but can be cultivated through practices that aim to recover its unconditioned quality. Traditionally, these involve disciplined attention to the body (including breathing), felt reactions, patterns of the mind, and apprehension of the basic nature of reality in all experience. Development of mindfulness in this way is a precondition of liberation, although other factors are required to complete the mental purification that permits this direct, immediate and irreversible knowledge of reality that in Buddhism is the only alternative to suffering. In practice, mindfulness is cultivated alongside closely related capacities such as clear comprehension. While these have not always been clearly distinguished, the synergies between mindfulness and the positive mental capacities it is most closely associated with in Buddhist psychology underpin the commonest ambiguities found in descriptions of 'mindfulness'.

Chapter 2

Understanding mindfulness: Science

> Not everything that can be counted counts, and not everything that counts can be counted.
>
> (sign in Albert Einstein's office at Princeton University)

Two and a half millennia after the elaboration of mindfulness within Buddhism, it should be possible to bring a considerable array of investigative methods to bear on questions posed in the previous chapter. These include what mindfulness is and how it affects the mind and body. For instance, if mindfulness is a distinct state of consciousness, it should be relatively straightforward to describe its characteristics in the same neurophysiological terms that have permitted differentiation of the various states of bodily and mental arousal associated with the different stages of sleep. Psychological science should be able to assist in the identification and measurement of experiences that characterise mindfulness, as well as clarifying what the consequences of the continued practice of mindfulness are likely to be.

Brain changes

The history of electrophysiological investigation of meditative states is a long but frankly disappointing one. The research has been scattered, methodologically inconsistent and poorly controlled. When reviewers comment on findings specific to 'mindfulness', they may be using the term idiosyncratically rather than in a way that makes for reliable comparison between one study and another. A huge amount of electrophysiological research on meditation took place in the 1970s and 1980s because of the popularity and claims of transcendental meditation (TM). This is a mantra-based meditation that is usually accompanied by states of deep relaxation. Classifiers of meditation tend to put it firmly in the category of 'concentrative' practices (e.g. Goleman 1988) on the basis of its subjective qualities. There was a need to distinguish TM's central effects from those of relaxation, and, despite counterclaims that it could not be associated with consistent findings (e.g. Pagano et al. 1976; Stigsby et al. 1981), it was widely associated with an increase in coherence on EEG recordings of frequencies in the alpha and theta ranges (e.g. Dilbeck and Bronson 1981; Gaylord et al. 1989). Such findings are not unique to TM, and Cloninger (2004) attributes changes of this kind to a state he terms 'mindfulness'. Cloninger points out how, in distinction from the alpha domination of drowsiness and the increasing beta activity that comes with ordinary wakefulness, higher conscious states are associated with co-occurring multiple frequencies, as well as greater coherence on the EEG trace. His state of 'mindfulness' is characterised by slow alpha (7–9 Hz) with theta in frontal cortical areas alongside less beta activity than in ordinary wakefulness. He also links these to early studies of changes in cerebral blood flow that suggest that mindfulness meditation is associated with greater blood flow to all three surfaces of the frontal lobe and the thalamus. He suggests that the former is consistent with inner focusing of attention and the latter to widespread if non-specific cortical activity.

Certainly, the most striking physiological findings in meditation research come from studies of experienced practitioners, when differences between aficionados of different traditions become more apparent. Probably the most famous – and suggestive – study to be conducted was Kasamatsu and Hirai's (1966) investigation of Soto Zen monks in Zazen meditation. As their meditation progressed, there was a tendency for alpha waves to increase in amplitude and then decrease in frequency, before theta waves appeared and grew in amplitude. The changes are more pronounced in monks of long experience (there was a subgroup with over 20 years' experience in their sample). Some of the most experienced meditators were subjected to a further investigation in which their responses to 20 clicks repeated at 15-second intervals were recorded and analysed. The finding that they failed to respond to repeated clicks by habituation of automatic responses, such as momentary blocking of alpha frequencies, seemed to suggest this was a demonstration of how, as a result of their training, they reacted to each stimulus as if they were hearing it for the first time. The experiment appeared to be a scientific demonstration of the 'beginner's mind' that is widely associated with mastery of Zen. (As noted in the previous chapter, this aspect of Zen is also reminiscent of mindful awareness.)

Tantalisingly, the study has never been satisfactorily repeated. An attempt to do so with TM meditators and yoga meditators of several years' experience showed both to habituate in ways comparable to untrained controls (Becker and Shapiro 1981). Even Zen meditators of seven and a half years' experience habituated – although, unlike the Soto monks, they meditated with their eyes closed! In reviewing the episode, Austin (1998) maintained that the monks in the original study were probably entering states of deep absorption that meant their brains were blocking the clicks, and any other external stimuli, at the subcortical level. However, Kasamatsu and Hirai's original report includes descriptions of the Zen masters' own experience during the investigation:

> [They] reported to us that they had more clearly perceived each stimulus than in their ordinary waking state. In this state of mind one cannot be affected by either external or internal stimulus, nevertheless he is able to respond to it. He perceives the object, responds to it, and yet is never disturbed by it . . . . One Zen master described such a state of mind as that of noticing every person one sees on the street but of not looking back with emotional curiosity.
>
> (Kasamatsu and Hirai 1966: 593)

Until a true replication is carried out, it seems impossible either to interpret the findings definitively or judge how relevant they are to the long-term impacts of mindfulness meditation.

Recent work with eight subjects having extensive experience of an objectless Tibetan meditation, in which their only action was to open themselves to feelings of pure compassion, has produced distinctive findings of a different kind (Lutz *et al.* 2004). It has involved careful analysis of rhythmic activity at faster frequencies than have usually been studied in previous work – the gamma range is around 40 cycles per second. While resting, these meditators were found to have significantly greater gamma band activity relative to slower activity than controls. This difference was greatly exacerbated during meditation periods. Examination of the power of the gamma activity, and the distances separating scalp electrode sites between which synchrony was evident, showed that both increased with the meditators' experience. Such long-distance synchrony is usually interpreted as the consequence of transient functional reorganisation in the brain, as neurons start to operate as a synchronised assembly rather than independently of one another. The implication is that, with the accumulation of meditative experience, a capacity for this organisation to occur over greater and greater areas develops. Lutz *et al.* report that gamma activity of the magnitude they report has not been seen in any other non-pathological group, meditators or non-meditators, while conceding such fast frequencies have not always been analysed in other studies. All future physiological studies of meditation clearly need to do so. In relating this work to other studies, observations that the raised gamma activity was most evident at prefrontal cortex and the insula are likely to be relevant.

In moving to mindfulness meditation, there are probably only three studies demonstrating sufficient clarity about the subjects' practice for them to be acceptable as studies of mindfulness rather than any other kind of practice. All are relatively recent. In the first, Dunn *et al.* (1999) set out to define electroencephalographic differences between relaxation, 'concentration' and 'mindfulness' meditations. Relaxation was equated with sitting comfortably with eyes closed; concentration was meditating while maintaining attention on the movements of the breath; mindfulness was allowing the attention to wander freely between events presenting to it, aiming to experience them clearly, and sometimes simultaneously labelling perceptions as 'seeing', 'hearing', feeling', etc. Concentration sessions would always take place while seated; mindfulness was practised while sitting and while walking. The 10 student subjects learned the two techniques in sequence (concentration before mindfulness) over 10 weeks. They continued some practice in concentration as they were learning mindfulness, but sessions and homework were tailored so that, by the end of training and prior to the crucial EEG recording sessions, they had an equal exposure to each (around 30 hours). EEG recordings were then conducted in all three conditions – the students indicating the depth of their experience in response to regular verbal prompts throughout the recording periods.

Comparisons were made between the three conditions in examining the distribution of activity across the scalp in each of five frequency bands. The plots of differences in activity during concentration compared to mindfulness showed significantly greater activity during mindfulness of four kinds: delta (left occipito-parietal and bilateral prefrontal); theta (left frontal); alpha (bilateral occipito-parietal), and beta 1 (i.e. 13–25 Hz) (left frontal and bilateral occipito-parietal). The fifth condition examined, termed beta 2 (25–37 Hz) by Dunn and colleagues, fell within the slowest part of the gamma spectrum. The picture there was much more mixed. Concentration recordings showed more activity over the occipital pole bilaterally, whereas at the frontal poles, there was significantly greater activity on the left during mindfulness and significantly greater activity on the right during concentration. There were also scattered areas of significant activity differences in parietal and right temporal locations at this frequency – with greater activity during mindfulness each time.

Dunn and colleagues (1999) felt the consistency of the differences here to be impressive, even if the findings during the mindfulness periods were counterintuitive at first glance. (Changes in slow-wave activity and fast-wave activity are usually complementary, rather than conjoint as here.) They reasoned that 'the brain is calm and relaxed, thereby producing more delta and theta waves, but is simultaneously awake and alert, thereby producing more alpha and beta 1 activity', so that 'the brain's electrophysiological response . . . coincides with the meditator's subjective report'. Dunn *et al.* believe their work is significant in resolving contradictions within the extensive literature on TM, where disparate and apparently contradictory findings all belong within the range of observations made within their study. This suggests that TM has had elements of both concentration and mindfulness, and they urge future researchers to study one or the other rather than continuing to confound the two. They also encourage others to continue to look at qualitative differences alongside quantitative measurements in future research.

The second notable study on mindfulness meditators was also a study on novice meditators. This time, mindfulness training was through participation in the full 8-week training of Jon Kabat-Zinn's mindfulness-based stress reduction (MBSR) (see Chapter 3). (Davidson *et al.* 2003) have undertaken a controlled study of the impact of an 8-week MBSR programme on brain activation. Here, 'activation' was assessed by computer analysis of electrical activity (brain electrical activity mapping), to monitor selectively the spectral power density of frequencies in the alpha range (8–13 Hz).

This is inversely proportional to the activation, with alpha activity being seen on a standard EEG when activation is not present. In the frontal lobes of the brain, asymmetrical activation, favouring one side more than the other, is consistently associated with specific mental states in the neurophysiology literature. For instance, greater left-sided activation has been associated with positive emotion. It has also been associated with enhanced immune function (measured in terms of natural killer cell activity), the other parameter in Davidson's study.

The brain activation and immune function of volunteers was assessed prior to commencement of MBSR, on completion of the course, and a further four months later. Sample records were always taken immediately after standard procedures to induce temporarily a positive mood and a negative mood. Immune function was assessed through influenza antibody titres. Results from the 25 subjects were compared with those of 16 controls. They did not differ significantly at the outset. The MBSR students differed from controls post-course, and at 4-month follow-up, with respect to greater anterior left–right asymmetry during both positive and negative mood induction. Their antibody titre was also significantly greater at these time points. When the variation within the sample was examined, a strong positive correlation between asymmetric activation and raised antibody titre was found, suggesting that frontal activation was directly linked to the improved immune response. Analysis of the distribution of the asymmetric activity found this to be stronger close to the midline rather than in the prefrontal region, as had been predicted.

Rather than speculate on the implications for localisation, Davidson noted the failure of these students to demonstrate significant improvement in positive affect as a possible reason why they did not show prefrontal differences also to the expected extent. An interesting observation is contained in a different report on the study (Goleman 2003: 345). The participants agreed to keep a record of their practice during the training period. These were not disclosed to Jon Kabat-Zinn, the instructor and co-researcher, until the sessions were concluded to ensure he was blind to this. Analysis of the post-MBSR brain activation and immunity status showed no correlation whatever with the time spent in mindfulness practice out of the training sessions. It is difficult to interpret this without independent corroboration of how 'mindful' each subject became. As it stands, the study could suggest that differences in post-training results reflected some students' greater capacity to switch into mindfulness during other tasks, rather than the impact of formal practice. Or it could support a contention that other variables, such as expectancy, are more important than practice of either kind in predicting outcome. Most of Davidson's other work on asymmetries of frontal activation has benefited from the higher resolution of functional magnetic resonance imaging (MRI). It will be extremely interesting to see how closely the variations within the EEG results are replicated in a functional MRI version of this study.

The third study, also controlled, has also attracted a good deal of press attention. Unusually, it was an anatomical, rather than a physiological, study, in which a possible link between the thickness of brain cortex and meditation experience was examined. The subjects were teachers and students of 'insight' meditation, characterised as 'mindful attention to internal and external stimuli' (Lazar et al. 2005: 1894). They had all attended retreats as well as practising regularly, with a minimum of 2 and an average of 9 years' experience. Because the subjects varied in the intensity of their practice, an additional measure to years of experience was used as an index of total meditative experience. This was respiration rate while sitting, which has been shown to decrease progressively with meditation experience in other studies. Measurements of cortical thickness for the 20 meditators were compared with 15 controls having no experience of meditation or yoga. The meditators' cortices were consistently thicker in several areas, in either hemisphere, but not thicker than the controls' cortices overall. Detailed comparisons were undertaken in areas hypothesised to be more likely to demonstrate effects from the existing literature and from the meditation's emphasis on sensory experience. These showed clear differences bilaterally in the prefrontal cortex (Brodmann areas 9 and 10) and around the right insula (including an area of auditory cortex). While differences in thickness were less clear across the groups at the right prefrontal cortex than the left, they were directly related to subjects' age. The older the subject, the greater the in-subject difference, suggesting that meditation might not be adding to the thickness here so much as preventing a thinning process that otherwise occurred naturally with age.

The study's other principal finding came from correlations between cortical thickness and meditation experience. Although these were not found in the prefrontal cortex, there was a part correlation with insular thickness after correcting for age, and a strong correlation only at an area of the inferior occipito-temporal visual cortex. Although the cross-sectional nature of the study compromises attempts to infer causality from these associations, it is being taken as evidence that meditative attention excites neuronal growth in brain areas likely to be activated in the course of meditation. No comparable studies have been conducted on practitioners from other meditative traditions. Assuming the findings can be replicated, it is unclear how specific they are to mindfulness meditation.

Measuring mindfulness with self-report questionnaires

Although at least seven questionnaires have been devised and undergone validation as measures of mindfulness, currently only three are published and properly in the public domain, with another being freely circulated. All attempt to provide some assessment of individuals' mindfulness from their responses to a paper self-report form. They differ significantly in their range of use, content and output.

The Mindful Attention and Awareness Scale (MAAS) (Brown and Ryan 2003) is a 15-item self-report questionnaire that has been widely distributed. The questions concern capacity to maintain attention and withstand distraction and were progressively selected from a huge pool on the basis of their lack of ambiguity, acceptability and discrimination. None of the questions refer to or are influenced by particular techniques of enhancing attention or awareness, in line with the authors' interest in exploring natural variation in 'mindfulness' irrespective of its origins. As it enquires about how well attention is maintained in some circumstances (e.g. while walking, eating or driving), and how far actions are undertaken automatically, it has high face and content validity for this construct. Responses to it yield a single score for capacity to maintain awareness. Scores have been shown to be greater among Zen meditators than non-meditating controls, but a study of medical patients designed to compare MAAS scores before and after MBSR training found no significant difference (Brown and Ryan 2003). This does not necessarily apply to other contexts, the authors proposing that the lack of change reflected unexpectedly high baseline scores that may be typical of this client group.

(Personal communications from other oncology professionals do suggest that present moment awareness is spontaneously enhanced among terminally ill people.)

Although the MAAS has been criticised for a perceived failure to measure a capacity for acceptance or non-judgement alongside attention and awareness, this was a deliberate decision. When working with a larger pool of candidate items for the scale, Brown and his colleagues found the correlation between scores for items reporting acceptance and those reporting attention was extremely high, as was the trend for them to move up or down in tandem. They found acceptance could be reliably inferred from the score for attention and awareness and did not need separate consideration.

The Toronto Mindfulness Scale (TMS) of Bishop *et al.* (2003) is quite different in nature and purpose. It set out to operationalise mindfulness as a state of mind reached through formal practice, so that apparent benefits following mindfulness-based interventions could be related directly to their psychological impact. Intended specifically for use with people suffering from emotional disorders, it was meant to check subjects' ability to prevent cognitive elaboration of experience as well as to maintain continuity of attention. It is designed to be filled in shortly after a mindfulness meditation session, and items refer specifically to experiences while attempting to meditate. The TMS is a compact scale of 10 items, which refer to recent awareness of internal sensations or thoughts, and the degree of reactivity that was shown toward these. The items were selected from a larger pool of candidate items as those that best discriminated experienced meditators from people with little or no experience of meditation. Factor analysis has confirmed that the items load to a single construct and the scale is scored to produce a single figure that, as an expression of mindfulness achieved *in situ*, could be taken as a measure of adherence to the meditation method. As befits a state measure, scores have been shown to fluctuate from session to session, with an overall tendency to rise according to experience. The instrument is currently unique as a method of assessing the direct contribution of (meditative) mindfulness practice in attainment of psychological change.

The Kentucky Inventory of Mindfulness Skills (KIMS) (Baer *et al.* 2004) was conceived within a different tradition of mindfulness training. The 'skills' referred to are primarily those identified by Marcia Linehan within the mindfulness training module of dialectical behaviour therapy (see Chapter 3). Four constructs that are prominent in mindfulness coaching within this model – observing, accepting without judgement, describing, and acting with awareness – have guided the initial selection of items, with further adjustments designed to minimise overlap between the sub-scales for each. A 39-item questionnaire has resulted that assesses each of these in terms of everyday habits of mind. It can therefore be used to assess aptitudes prior to any training in mindfulness skills, as well as to assess changes once this has been undertaken.

The Freiburg Mindfulness Inventory (FMI) (Buchheld *et al.* 2002) is another self-report measure that yields a single score, although its conceptual structure is relatively complex. Choice of its 30 items was guided by experienced vipassana meditators' views of what mindfulness is. They were placed by the authors under four headings following a factor analysis: 'present-moment disidentify-ing attention'; 'nonjudgemental, nonevaluative attitude toward self and others'; 'openness to negative mind states'; and 'process-orientated, insightful understanding'. The FMI is longer estab-lished than the other measures here, and the scope of its questions is broader than in any other instrument. The first of its factors is itself broad and, as its title suggests, actually embraces items that would usually be seen now as indicative of distinct facets of mind-fulness. The acuity of awareness (as in 'I sense my body, whether eating, cooking, cleaning or talking') and non-reactivity (as in 'I watch my feelings without becoming lost in them') sit side by side within this factor. Unlike the other scales, the FMI deliberately includes features that are assumed to increase as a consequence of attaining greater 'mindfulness' rather than being components of it. (This accounts for most items under the scale's other three subheadings.) The FMI has been shown to discriminate clearly between experienced and inexperienced meditators, but it may not recommend itself so easily to those researchers who would see the links between attentive processes and their consequences as a subject for further investigation, rather than as something that a measure of mindfulness should assess at the same time.

Some interrelationships and complementarities between these measures will be evident from these descriptions. Important ques-tions arise about how far the scales do measure the same things, and, collectively, how well they reflect the semantic scope of 'mind-fulness'. Ruth Baer (2006) has investigated these questions by a comparative study of five questionnaires, in which they were jointly administered to a large sample of students. This allowed study of the intercorrelation of scores from the different instruments as routinely applied, as well as factor analysis of the pooled items from all the questionnaires. The questionnaires concerned were the FMI, MAAS and KIMS as well as two unpublished measures. These were a 12-item 'Cognitive Affective Mindfulness Scale' (CAMS), reportedly very similar in structure and scope to the KIMS, and a 10-item Mindfulness Questionnaire (MQ), developed for use with patients with psychosis, which reportedly emphasises reactivity to negative experiences. The Toronto Mindfulness Scale was not included in the published study. This has meant that the available item pool had a heavy weighting toward items from the KIMS and the CAMS, instruments that place the naming of experiences and acting with mindfulness on a par with aspects such as the immediacy of awareness or being accepting.

Factor analysis led to a five-factor solution, initially accounting for only 33 per cent of the variance. (The low proportion of the total variance here may be partly explained by the lack of meditation experience among the sample.) This structure informed the selection of those items having the highest exclusive correlation with each of the five factors, to yield a new composite 39-item instrument, the Five Factors Mindfulness Questionnaire (FFMQ). These factors were observing, non-judging, non-reactivity, describing and acting mindfully. This is essentially the same structure as Baer's own KIMS, with the addition of 'non-reactivity'. There are no items from the KIMS in this non-reactivity subscale, which is indebted to the FMI and MQ for its questions about being untroubled and undistracted by negative experiences. However, inspection suggests that differences between this subscale and the non-judging one may reflect the use of terminology in the KIMS, which dominates the latter, rather than substance. Unlike the FMI, the KIMS tends to enquire about reactions to experiences in terms of making judgements following them, rather than about accepting them. Items from the MAAS retained within the FFMQ were weighted almost exclusively on the 'acting mindfully' factor, alongside some further items from the KIMS.

These details are mentioned because the history of this apparently comprehensive instrument's development is important when appreciating areas of possible weakness. Baer (2006) has subsequently gone on to use the FFMQ in a much needed study of experienced meditators. In an ambitious series of investigations, she has attempted to link meditative experience to measures of psychological functioning, and to facets of mindfulness, and to seek evidence for the mediation of any associations between meditation and psychological functioning by mindfulness. Her sample this time has included very experienced mindfulness practitioners – 19 per cent having 10 years or more experience. However, although all of the facets assessed by the FFMQ correlate with at least some of the indices of positive psychological functioning that were used, the data linking meditation experience to aspects of mindfulness were quite unequivocal. Only observation and non-reactivity showed truly robust associations with meditation experience. Stratification of this sample according to their reported experience has permitted a preliminary analysis of how far attainments on either observation or non-reactivity correspond to meditative experience. It appears from this that observation steadily improves in quality from the start of training, whereas non-reactivity is a later development. There are, of course, inherent limitations to this kind of cross-sectional survey, which can be reduced by observing how a pre-identified set of practitioners change over time through a planned series of assessments.

It is worth commenting a little further here on the content validity of these measures – that is, whether they appear to measure what they are supposed to from the questions they ask – in the light of the examination of mindfulness in Chapter 1. There are certainly kinds of experience that are mentioned there, and that are traditionally associated with mindfulness, that are encountered only in the FMI. These include feeling tranquil and being curious about what is happening (with respect to emotions and actions, if not sensations). The FMI is also the only instrument to mention some aspects of what Shapiro *et al.* (2006) would classify as 'attitude', such as 'friendliness'. There are still other ways in which the content of the FMI differs from other instruments. It pays considerable attention to respondents' relationship to their own thoughts through items such as '2. I know that I am not identical to my thoughts'. While this kind of item does not appear in any other instrument, even the FFMQ, it is a precise description of one of the two things Kabat-Zinn reports being most valued by his students (Salzberg and Kabat-Zinn 1997). Curiously, the other consequence that Kabat-Zinn reports as being most valued does not figure in any of the instruments! It is subtle and best expressed in his own words:

They have a new-found awareness of the special quality of breath that relates to a greater sensitivity and awareness of their whole body. Along with the breath comes a sense of greater appreciation for the miracle of having a body, even if the body has a disability. Each breath, each moment, is a miracle, and when you begin to experience that directly, it vitalizes the quality of your life.

(Salzberg and Kabat-Zinn 1997: 141)

If the FMI's 30 questions manage to tap a relatively broad range of practitioners' experience, this may reflect both its origins in wide consultation with experienced meditators, and the relative unimportance of theory in determining its structure.

Baer's most recent work, despite giving constructs such as 'mindful action' or 'describing' a generous opportunity to establish their place, seems to confirm instead that the two most measurable aspects of mindfulness using self-report scales correspond to maintaining an open, present awareness (observing) and an accepting attitude (non-reactivity). This is consistent with a 'proposed operational definition' devised by members of a well-established research group in Toronto (Bishop *et al.* 2004). Baer has been able to compare the scores on these two dimensions from the FFMQ across her sample of experienced meditators when it is stratified according to their experience. This indicates that the quality of observation grows progressively in the expected direction from early in a meditator's practice, while there is usually no change in non-reactivity until an initial lag period has been completed (Baer 2006). The likelihood of such a difference should generate prospective studies, in which a cohort of starting students is followed up at regular intervals, as this is the only reliable way to obtain an accurate picture of the dynamic relationship between these factors.

Unfortunately, it remains unclear what the most sensitive way of measuring them may be. Among the traditional published questionnaires, it is only the oldest instrument, the FMI, that contains many items that correspond to each of these factors. Within its own structure, however, they are not clearly distinguished. All of the items that have become indicators of 'nonreactivity' in Baer's FFMQ come under 'present-moment disidentifying attention' in the FMI. The four items signalling 'observing' in the FFMQ are divided evenly between 'present-moment disidentifying attention' and 'openness to negative mind states' on the FMI. In summary, if it is slightly clearer what the questions need to be to tap these two dimensions of mindful experience, much work remains to devise an instrument whose internal structure is clearly preferable to any alternative.

Recent studies are producing some confirmation that, whatever else it is, mindfulness appears to represent a capacity that can be coached and that usually follows a developmental curve. In order to assess where somebody may be on such a trajectory, it is essential to have a reliable set of images not of mindfulness as a single capacity, but as something that may have distinct properties as someone acquires more experience with it. People belonging to either end of this spectrum may, operationally, appear to have very little in common, as the neurophysiological studies reviewed at the start of the chapter seemed to suggest.

Understanding mindfulness through qualitative research

Two things are evident to date from efforts to research the impacts of mindfulness-based interventions, especially MBSR, by quantitative methods. One is that, for any study that links practice of MBSR to a given outcome, evidence will be needed that this apparent effect results from subjects becoming more mindful as a result of the MBSR intervention. Many of the early studies contained no 'marker' of mindfulness that would serve this purpose, while there has been a good deal of activity recently to introduce and validate scalar self-report measures that could have this function. However, attempts to objectify 'mindfulness' by reducing it to elements such as skills in receptivity, sustained attention, awareness of internal sensations, awareness of other sensations or thoughts, acting mindfully, being non-judgemental, and so forth only highlight a lack of consensus about what it is to be 'mindful' – as well as indicating possible limits imposed by a need to quantify the result.

In general, qualitative research can be helpful in several ways when scoping a (psychological) research area. Done well, it will first of all indicate the range of experiences that are likely to be encountered when investigating an area. Secondly, it will indicate how much variation in the findings arises through idiosyncrasy. Thirdly, it can help to account for such variation by its ability to contextualise the content of individuals' reports in terms of life circumstances or other individual factors, permitting explanation. Fourth, by indicating elements that are common across individual accounts, but which may require redescription, it can help to shape a conceptual framework and thereby contribute to the theorisation of a topic. Individual studies are now being performed in order to understand the needs of, and likely impacts on, specific client groups when undertaking interventions like the MBSR programme (e.g. Mason and Hargreaves 2001). However, the continuing failure to utilise qualitative research methods in the articulation of mindfulness within psychology remains, in my view, mindless.

As an illustration of the potential of qualitative research, I shall draw on an exploratory study I conducted some years ago based on a single focus group with six people with an active mindfulness practice. The five women and one man all had significant personal experiences of mindfulness teaching and practice. The discussion was recorded by audio tape, and a full transcript made for subsequent analysis. The discussion was organised around four questions, discussed by the group in turn. At each stage, members were encouraged to illustrate their comments with personal experience. The four guiding questions were:

1   What makes an experience mindful?
2   How does practice of MBSR reduce 'stress'?
3   How does mindfulness develop over time?
4   Are there any negative consequences of mindfulness practice?

It should be said the process of the group was, in itself, remarkable. Some members were known to others, but there was an impressive curiosity concerning all the contributions that were made. Occasionally, a member's observations did not chime with others' experience, but this would be noted with respect and interest and an absence of argument. Although the question sequence had been prepared beforehand, only the first question was explicitly asked in advance of the group taking it up for discussion. For the other three questions, the group moved seamlessly through the sequence, being advised when they had anticipated the next question, while continuing to contribute occasional observations on earlier questions as they went on reflecting during the session. At the end of the discussion, the members expressed considerable appreciation of what they had heard and learned from each other.

Another comment is essential. At the time of the study, I remained personally naive to the literature that is being quoted throughout this book, with the exception of three practice-focused books. There was no wish to box or categorise the findings according to prevalent theories of mindfulness, including those I have summarised from the traditional literature. Accordingly, at the time of the study, it was necessary to coin some neologisms to describe phenomena that were clearly salient but unnamed in the discussion, rather than borrow terms from other contexts. In summarising it here, I have also not changed any of the terminology that arose within those original analyses.

The transcript was subjected to more than one analysis. In the first, the questions were used to organise the members' comments as responses to one or more of the questions – a thematic content analysis. The themes this identified were aggregated into larger themes when there was demonstrable overlap, before their relative salience was assessed through the frequency with which they appeared as verbal comments and the extent to which they stimulated affirmative comments from other group members. This has been written up in detail elsewhere (Mace 2006), but a brief summary follows, highlighting its implications for the present discussion.

Characteristics of 'mindfulness'

In addressing the first question, 'What makes an experience mindful?', all of the contributors retrospectively recognised continuity between experiences that had been part of mindfulness training, and others that had preceded these. The commonest example of this was yoga, but two of the participants with musical experience spoke with feeling and in detail about the performance and practice of (Western classical) music as a meditative and mindful practice. Another participant had experience of the Alexander technique and saw this as cultivating a mindful attitude through its emphasis on awareness. In discussion, the participants were encouraged to discriminate between the characteristics of a 'mindful' experience, and other kinds of meditative experience that, in their experience, were not truly mindful. This was a productive move, helped by the participants having a variety of other meditative experiences on which to draw. These were not investigated in detail, but half the group referred to prior experience with the mantra-based technique of TM. This helped the following distinctions to be drawn:

1   Mindfulness as *inclusive* awareness. In comparison with TM, mindfulness meditation led to a sense of expanded awareness that embraced many domains – not only mental and physical sensations but the room in which meditation was taking place.
2   Mindfulness as retaining a sense of self. The sense of self was not attenuated to the extent it had been for those who had participated in other meditations and experienced a loss of personal agency during them. There was not complete consensus on this point.
3   Mindfulness specifically includes the body. One participant felt this was the crucial distinction between mindful meditation and other meditations (including TM); the others agreed.

Five more characteristics of mindfulness emerged as members thought about what, for them, made an experience 'mindful':

1   a single-minded attention to what was present to the exclusion of anything else
2   an equanimity that accompanies this attention
3   a suspension of attempts to control the experience, or letting be
4   disidentification from thoughts – the sense that a thought can be changed and can be let go of was felt to be an especially helpful aspect of mindfulness practice
5   being able to rely on spontaneous actions in everyday life.

Reducing stress with mindfulness

The thing members of this group most clearly shared had been experience of MBSR. And there was no doubting that they each found themselves better able to deal with stress in their personal lives. The topic was raised in the discussion in order to discover how they did this in practice. Participants referred to experiences of psychological stress, especially fear, even more than experience of somatic pain. A wide range of pain experiences were cited, from coping with dental pain to chronic pain. Removal of fear was emphasised in this context. In discussion of situations where an illness was potentially terminal, stress was identified most closely with the fears of not knowing what would happen and of dying. The specific techniques that members used to reduce stress when faced by situations reflected different aspects of mindfulness. A participant who had emphasised the value of realising that thoughts were just thoughts commented on the value of this in reducing stress. Under more extreme threats, there would be a reappraisal of priorities, which brought with it a determination to value each moment. The specific techniques used in straightforward circumstances, such as the dental chair, involved deliberate attention to the breath and to sensations in the body using the 'body scan' of MBSR. In facing unnerving situations with other people, a technique falling outside standard MBSR teaching was cited that instilled positive feelings in place of fear prior to meetings. Participants confirmed that their preparedness grew with continuing practice of mindfulness techniques.

Progressive effects of mindfulness

Like its application in the face of stress, other aspects of mindfulness might be expected to deepen with practice and cumulative experience. The discussion identified some that appeared only to emerge as the result of sustained practice. One group of these were closely interrelated, being ways in which the experience of mindfulness spread beyond its initial, intended scope. I called them aspects of the 'permeation' of mindfulness, a term used and appreciated during the group's discussion. Permeation was seen in an infiltration of mindfulness across an increasing range of activities of daily living, but also in a progressive growth in the continuity of awareness throughout the day and in the increasing spontaneity of mindful experience, such that it arose more and more without deliberate intention.

The other emergent aspects of mindfulness to be reported were a new sensitivity to others (a sense of being more sensitively attuned to them, which was also increasingly recognised by those other people) and a range of positive feelings that participants appeared to experience more regularly. These feelings included an unshakeable sense of trust in life, a deepening (but light-hearted) compassion, and a sense of profound love. These were spoken about as if they were far from incidental, but were now core to the participants' experience of mindfulness. At the same time, there was a sense that mindfulness could not and should not be about doing things, but was simply about being with life as it happened.

Negative consequences of mindfulness

In the final stage of the discussion, and only then, were comments about possible negative consequences of mindfulness practice invited. In response, participants either recounted experiences when they were new to formal mindfulness practice, or when they had meditated intensively in a retreat setting. The initial problems were in the form of discomfort and, more interestingly, of living with the guilt of failing to live up to their own resolutions and expectations. There was also an admission of intolerance of others who were unwilling to take up mindfulness practice when it seemed likely to help them. Subsequently, members volunteered some ambivalent feelings about becoming acquainted with more difficult aspects of their personality in the course of practice, and about calling a halt on cherished projects as a greater realism set in. However, the consequences of these realisations did not appear to have been sources of serious or lasting regret. Difficulties were consistently spoken of as a challenge that needed to be embraced with equanimity within further practice. Negative experiences from participation in intensive retreats were more acute. Two members described vivid perceptual alterations that had been short-lived – and apparently responsive to being made the object of mindful attention.

In keeping with good practice in qualitative research, I had abstained from detailed examination of relevant literature until coding and analysis of the transcript had been completed. Subsequent comparison of the group members' reports with the current literature on the assessment of mindfulness indicated which aspects of their experience were most remarkable – at least in relation to the aspects of mindfulness that quantitative research had already highlighted.

Of the six qualities that prompted subjects to see an experience as 'mindful', both inclusiveness and single-mindedness are consistent with statements that mindful attention is non-selective and fully engaged. The qualities of 'equanimity' and 'letting be' appear to reflect the 'acceptance' or 'non-reactivity' that is now emerging as a constituent of mindful attention (Bishop *et al.* 2004; Brown and Ryan 2004). The remaining observations concerning 'disidentification from thoughts' and 'spontaneous actions' indicate areas that have also been recognised in some attempts to operationalise mindfulness, but not others. Disidentification from thoughts was being described in terms identical with its description in the

FMI and the TMS, or indeed the concept of cognitive 'decentering' (Safran and Segal 1990) on which items of the latter were based. Spontaneous action is close to the skill of 'acting mindfully' that Linehan (1993a) emphasised and that was intentionally represented in the KIMS, CAMS and FFMQ (and probably, in practice, in the MAAS).

Many of the comparisons these participants made between other meditative experiences and mindful ones are also reflected in the literature on psychological mindfulness. Although group members spoke about mindful awareness as embracing all forms of experience, including awareness of external as well as internal objects, it will be clear from the descriptions provided previously that self-report measures differ considerably in the range of experience they enquire about. However, all of the mindfulness scales that were reviewed do include reference to awareness of body sensations. As these were the most 'mindful' kind of focus the group recognised when differentiating meditative experiences as mindful from their content, that emphasis seems sound.

The group's members had little difficulty in responding to the invitation to differentiate between aspects of their experience that are quickly realisable ('common') and those that emerge with the passage of years ('emergent'). Until the very recent questionnaire-based studies summarised above, the impact of previous practice on the experience of mindfulness has been relatively unexplored in questionnaire-based studies, despite the considerable evidence of its importance from the studies of neurophysiology and psychological functioning cited elsewhere in this chapter. When the existing scalar measures have been deliberately designed to differentiate between experienced and inexperienced practitioners, they have done this by identifying mindfulness skills that were expected to be common to all practitioners, but could become more developed with experience. The FMI is notable in attempting to do this, thereby including many items that have been interpreted as the consequences of mindful practice, rather than integral to mindfulness.

The FMI has several items on positive attitude to self (e.g. 'I am friendly to myself when things go wrong'), while the MAAS, FMI and TMS have items corresponding to different aspects of what I have labelled 'permeation'. All three invite observations on the range and continuity of attention, but only the FMI appears able to tap the spontaneity of mindful experience (e.g. 'I experience moments of inner peace and ease, even when things get hectic and stressful'). 'Attunement to others' remains as a characteristic recognised by members of the focus group that does not feature in any of the principal mindfulness measures. (Among the scales, only the FMI makes any reference to other people. This is a single item which checks how far the respondent becomes impatient with others.) As one of the criticisms that have been made of mindfulness-based therapeutic approaches is their apparent neglect of personal relations (e.g. Horowitz 2002), this seems an omission of strategic as well as descriptive importance.

Apart from relating, it was the more emotional aspects of mindfulness, as experienced by this group, such as emergent love and compassion, that had least place in any of the scalar measures. Conversely, the FMI also includes elements that were not prominent in this group's discussion, nor in the content of other scales. Examples include transience ('I am aware how brief and fleeting my experience is') and metacognition ('I consider things from different perspectives'; 'I pay attention to what's behind my actions'). Interestingly, these items have been among those least able to find a stable place within that scale's internal factor structure (Buchheld et al. 2002), suggesting either that, when they do occur, they are somewhat accidental and unnecessary aspects of mindfulness – or that they may themselves be emergent aspects, likely to be found with increasing experience, that were not picked up in this exploratory qualitative study.

In terms of the systematic study of mindfulness, this exercise, despite its many limitations, has at least one implication that cannot be ignored. This is that proper qualitative exploration of the range of the phenomenon under study needs to precede and to underpin attempts to derive validated scalar measures. This is good practice in other fields of psychological research: it is ironic just how much it has been ignored in investigations of this most introspective phenomenon.

In addition, more detailed coding was undertaken in order to explore the hidden structure of the conversation in more depth by techniques borrowed from grounded theory (Strauss and Corbin 1990; Charmaz 2001) in a finer grained, 'bottom-up' approach. This identified themes in the material irrespective of the questions that had guided the discussion. Units (nodes) of meaning were identified whenever the content of conversation could be labelled by a concept mentioned by one of the speakers, yielding 88 distinct nodes. Their semantic relationships were then explored with the assistance of a dedicated software program (NVivo 2.0) (Gibbs 2002), leading to their arrangement within a progressive, hierarchical structure. When nodes could not be completely subsumed under others, they would be grouped under more abstract, axial nodes within a tree structure. Progressive reiteration identified an implicit internal structure for the group's conversation, orientated around three independent axial nodes near the top of the tree structure: mindfulness, illness, and self/identity. These subsumed every other theme.

By continuing the investigation to its logical conclusion, according to the rules of procedure of 'grounded theory' (Charmaz 2001), it was possible to identify a single, implicit construct lying at the apex of the conceptual hierarchy. All of the discussion's content was in effect an elaboration of this central theory. The construct that emerged was 'embodiment'.

Apart from its implications for future quantitative investigations, what does an exploratory study of this kind tell us? The first, thematic analysis is sufficient to indicate that more qualities were being identified with 'mindfulness' than the questionnaires had acknowledged. A single group discussion is unlikely to be exhaustive in this respect. A full study should subject groups of different participants drawn from the same population to the same process until a new group fails to produce any new themes. Only at this point, termed 'saturation', is it reasonable to conclude that the groups have provided an adequate exploration of the scope of 'mindfulness'. It is possible that, by doing this, additional observations, such as metacognition and friendliness, which have been incorporated into items on the FMI, would be added to the pool. Or they may not come into the pool, even when saturation is reached, because they express a way of understanding mindfulness that is not represented here, with the possibility that there are irreducible differences between one population's experience of mindfulness and another's. (The plausibility of this is evident from the distinctiveness of Ellen Langer's work. This presents a non-Buddhistic conception of 'mindfulness' that equates it exclusively with metacognitive skills such as seeing a problem from many sides (cf. Langer 1989). Even within the range of usage being considered in this book, Shapiro et al.'s (2006) formulation of mindfulness as the resultant of intention and attitude, as well as attention, would make consistent differences more likely, as both intention and attitude are likely to differ from one training system to another.)

If mindfulness has a particular flavour that is common to practitioners of, say, MBSR, but that is not shared by practitioners of, say, vipassana meditation, then the second, grounded theory, mode of analysis provides a way of articulating the difference in terms of the core focus of either practice. It remains to be seen whether the centrality of embodiment holds for all mindful practices, or whether it is characteristic of MBSR. The specifics of MBSR will be covered more fully in the next chapter, alongside some other widely used ways of bringing mindfulness into clinical practice. Since I inferred embodiment to be the central theory of the group's discussion from these analytic procedures, nothing in my subsequent experience of MBSR has seemed inconsistent with its being the organising principle of that method.

The psychological impact of mindfulness: evidence from projective testing

The need for a truly satisfactory measure of mindfulness is growing, now that tentative evidence is amassing to challenge Bishop's (2002) observation that there is no objective evidence that mindfulness training has its effects because trainees' mindfulness increases. Work seems likely to continue on its mediating role between mindfulness training and observed clinical effects, and into different psychological factors that change subsequent to mindfulness training. However, these risk being pressed into the service of explaining why mindfulness might have a particular effect through a particular process, rather than a more fundamental enquiry into the nature of the overall psychological change mindfulness might bring about. If the traditional theories examined in Chapter 1 have any basis, these effects are likely to be very wide-ranging, influencing many aspects of experience at the same time. One way in which this has been expressed, in both classical Buddhist literature and modern psychology, is in terms of mindfulness meditation reversing the mind's conditioning.

A pioneering investigation of this was undertaken by Brown and Engler (1986) in the 1970s. The intention was to compare mental functioning as it was manifest in perceptual and cognitive processes by getting meditators to respond to the kind of projective psychological tests used in the analysis of personality and psychic conflict in the 1960s and 1970s. These were to include the famous Rorschach test, in which a series of 10 ink blots are presented with an invitation to give free associations to them. Brown and Engler used three subject groups: American meditators attending an intensive 3-month retreat, very experienced American meditators whose practice was rated by teachers as 'deep', and a group of Burmese meditators and their teachers. The latter were included as all were said to be in a recognised state of enlightenment. (They are a most interesting group, in that far from being monks, all the students were wives or mothers whose enlightenment experience came within 3 years of starting meditation and whose retreat experience was typically much less than that of the American 'beginners'.) Before any analysis of their performance on projective testing, the sample was classified, not according to their background or known meditative experience, but by an assessment of their level of meditative attainment. For this, the following five stages of attainment were identified (consistent with previous theoretical studies by Brown): beginners, concentration (*samadhi*) group, insight group, advanced insight group, and masters (this last occupied by a single teacher from the South Asian sample). The classification of each student was made through a combination of consensus between at least two expert teachers, and the student's answers to questions from a scale previously developed by the investigators (and now unobtainable), the Profile of Meditative Experience (POME). This inventory contained no fewer than 600 questions, apparently culled from classic manuals like the *Visuddhimagga* (Buddhaghosa 1999) as well as the training provided to contemporary teachers of meditation. These comprised signposts of people's meditative attainment, allowing them to be placed in one of the above categories on the basis of their reported experiences.

The result was that the largest group, beginning students, divided into 15 who remained beginners after a 3-month retreat, 13 who were seen as attaining concentration but not insight, and only three who had attained the direct 'insight' necessary for admission to the third stage. These three were distinguished from their co-retreatants by having at least 5 years' previous meditative experience. The other eight Americans who were invited to join the study by virtue of the recognised depth of their experience divided equally into the 'insight' and 'advanced insight' groups after assessment. The only member of the master's group was from South Asia. All the other South Asian participants, despite the relative brevity of the experience of most, were categorised as having 'advanced insight' after assessment. Apart from raising important questions about the relative amenability of this meditative tradition to people from different cultures, the other nine Burmese participants made no active contribution to the study. Despite the labour that went into translating the POME into the participants' home language, the authors felt the difficulties of 'cross-cultural Rorschach interpretation' precluded reporting of their test results.

This may appear to be an unfortunate decision, as the quite detailed reports provided on the performances of other participants are remarkable, with clearly discernible and apparently consistent differences according to group membership. The Rorschach tests of retreatants who remained in the beginners' group did not meaningfully differ from the tests they had completed prior to the retreat. Those who entered the concentration group made responses that were notable for their 'unproductivity and paucity of associative elaborations'. They complained that the investigators' demands that they associate in an elaborative way would take their energy and require the reassembly of perceptual layers that had broken down. At the same time, they were acutely aware of the physical features of the ink blot, seeing it as an ink blot, and commenting on its shape, colour and textures. If they did respond to the invitation to elaborate with other images, these were reported as being very fluid and quickly changing, while the subject would be curious about the internal process through which this was happening.

The Rorschach tests from the ex-retreatants and invitees that made up the insight group were remarkable for their 'increased productivity and richness of associative elaborations', as if there was a freeing up of associative processes and the subjects' imaginations. As these subjects talk freely and metaphorically about the blots' characteristics and the emotional responses these induced, the authors note how the developing narratives were always very responsive to what can be seen, commenting on this as evidence of the subjects' 'enhanced reality attunement'. The narratives could have a very life-affirming content, while, when subjected to the intrepretative techniques ordinarily used to rate the tests, showing evidence of personal psychological conflict over sexual or aggressive impulses.

The small 'advanced insight' group yielded three Rorschach tests that the authors found to be different again, yet very consistent. They are described as apparently more ordinary than the previous two groups at first sight. While they are productive as in the insight group, it is in a less divergent way, and this is combined with an attention to physical characteristics and perceived movement reminiscent of the concentration group's responses. What marks them out, however, is a repeated tendency by three of the four subjects in this group to 'perceive the ink blots as an interaction of form and energy or form and space'. This means that the ink blot would be seen as energy or space rather than as ink, while the subjects were commenting about the perception having distinct but interrelated levels. Their comments about energy and space would relate to the form of the ink blots, but be elaborated in a discourse about their systemic relationships to other energic or spatial entities in a world where matter is seen as movement. The authors comment here too from a conventional psychological perspective on the subjects' unusually undefended attitude to depictions of personal difficulties that would ordinarily be the source of much internal conflict.

The only Rorschach test from a 'master' was also the only one considered from an Asian subject. At no point did he talk about the ink blot as anything other than a projection of the mind. Furthermore, having no prior experience of the test, the master used the 10 ambiguous images to produce a cogent discourse on the Buddha's teaching concerning the ending of human suffering that linked all of the images in the sequence in which they had been presented. Accordingly, the early cards portrayed different kinds of suffering, and midsequence ones the mental habits that perpetuate it, before the later cards became depictions of the process of liberation and its freeing consequences. Throughout, the master incorporated features of each blot in the choice of images for his narrative, being particularly sensitive to gradations of shading.

Projective tests have fallen into general disfavour as a means of psychological diagnosis. Their interpretative schemes have been very dependent on psychoanalytic theory, and their very ambiguity raises concerns about reliability when used in clinical testing. However, instruments such as the Rorschach blots, or the pictorial story stems used in the Thematic Apperception Test that Murray and Morgan developed in the 1930s, provide methods of eliciting projected mental contents in research contexts independent of any interpretative schema. If mindfulness has an impact on the organisation of perceptual experience, there seems no reason why instruments of this kind should not be used in further studies across other samples of Western meditators encompassing a broader range of experience and accomplishment.

All four kinds of study that have been examined here – physiological, questionnaire-based, qualitative, and projective – currently suffer from a similar problem. Inconsistencies in methods, sampling or both mean that none can yet claim to demonstrate what that methodology is likely to reveal about mindfulness when investigated under optimal conditions.

Conclusions

Our understanding of mindfulness can be assisted by scientific investigations in several ways. Attempts to link mindfulness with specific brain states should be helped by advances in the resolution of functional imaging techniques. They have been limited by a lack of clarity in the discrimination of different meditation-related subjective states. It is also evident from empirical studies that 'mindfulness' is not static. Its apparent characteristics reflect at least the length (and probably the intensity) of an individual's practice. Further work is required to distinguish the psychological features that are intrinsic to mindfulness and those that represent its sequelae. There are reasons to suspect that 'mindfulness' is not necessarily a unitary phenomenon, even if progressive effects are taken into account. As there could be irreducible differences between one system of training and another, further qualitative investigations should be helpful. Attempts to devise scales that measure mindfulness have been hampered by the failure to take practitioners' experience into account, as well as a collective reluctance to inform their design by exploratory qualitative studies into the range of relevant phenomena. More work on each of these apparently disparate frontiers is needed if future scientific investigation of mindfulness is to be coherent and productive.

Chapter 3

Mindful therapy

> The faculty of bringing back a wandering attention over and over
> again is the very root of judgment, character and will. No-one is
> *compos sui* if he have it not. An education which should improve
> this faculty would be *the* education *par excellence*.
>
> (James 1927: 95)

The traditional aims and methods of mindfulness practice were
introduced in Chapter 1. Its application to the whole field of mental
health has depended upon the use of mindfulness within psychological treatments used to alleviate mental suffering. These take a
variety of forms, in which the contribution of mindfulness may be
covert as well as explicit. This chapter surveys the growing range of
therapeutic approaches that are bringing mindfulness to bear on
emotional difficulties. The scope of these is potentially vast, and
where it is necessary to give greater priority to some than others,
this will reflect their availability (particularly within public mental
health services) and theoretical significance.

Mindfulness in psychodynamic therapies

Incorporation of mindfulness into psychotherapeutic techniques
moves attention to the heart of psychotherapy. Given that psychotherapy depends so heavily upon the interaction between therapist
and patient, it is remarkable how little prominence attention has
received in its clinical literature. Notable exceptions have included
Freud, who believed psychoanalysts' attention was essential to their
practice. According to him, the psychoanalyst should maintain

evenly hovering attention . . . all conscious exertion is to be
withheld from the capacity for attention, and one's 'unconscious memory' is to be given full play; or to express it in terms
of technique, pure and simple: one has simply to listen and not
to trouble to keep in mind anything in particular. [Failure to
do this risks] never finding anything but what he already
knows.

(Freud 1912: 111–12)

There is a nuance in the German *gleichshwebende Aufmerksamkeit*
that makes it important that the translation is 'evenly hovering'
attention, rather than 'evenly suspended' attention. Not only is
attention being kept back in a very alert condition, but it is being
evenly spread as it hovers across the field of experience. While
Freud's injunction is deceptively simple, it is very hard to realise in
practice. The temptation to leap from quietly gathering clarity to
an interpretative declaration that has the effect of dispelling it
again can be irresistible. The subsequent history of 'evenly hovering attention' was for the concept to become distorted in the hands
of Freud's immediate successors. As Epstein (1984) relates, instructions to suspend judgement and theorisation were transformed into
a justification for partial if apparently spontaneous interpretations
on the part of the analyst.

Possibly in reaction to this, an equally famous call for
psychoanalysts to refine their own attentive processes came from
the British psychoanalyst Wilfred Bion in his *Attention and
Interpretation*:

The capacity to forget, the ability to eschew desire and understanding, must be regarded as essential discipline for the
psycho-analyst. Failure to practise this discipline will lead to a
steady deterioration in the powers of observation whose main-
tenance is essential. The vigilant submission to such discipline
will by degrees strengthen the analyst's mental powers just in
proportion as lapses in this discipline will debilitate them.

(Bion 1970: 51–2)

Bion's concern was that the analyst does not squander his or her
attention in the observation of phenomena that, for Bion, are

ultimately only distractions. The point of the essential discipline he refers to is that consciousness does not become what he terms 'saturated':

> If the psycho-analyst has allowed himself the unfettered play of memory, desire, and understanding, his pre-conceptions will be habitually saturated and his 'habits' will lead him to resort to instantaneous and well-practised saturation from 'meaning' rather than from O.
>
> (Bion 1970: 51)

Whereas Freud's instructions seem compatible with traditional methods for attaining 'bare attention', this is less clear with Bion. For instance, Bion insisted that attention be withdrawn from not only 'memory, desire and understanding' but also sense perceptions:

> Freud . . . speaks of blinding himself artificially. As a method of achieving this artificial blinding I have indicated the importance of eschewing memory and desire. Continuing and extending the process, I include understanding and sense perception with the properties to be eschewed. The suspension of memory, desire, understanding, and sense impressions may seem to be impossible without a complete denial of reality; but the psycho-analyst is seeking something that differs from what is normally known as reality.
>
> (Bion 1970: 43)

In fact, Bion wishes to develop a faculty he calls 'intuition' to arrive at extrasensory apprehensions of a psychic reality that is beyond words and that he refers to as 'O'. He often refers to this process as F or 'faith', while insisting it is just as dependable as logic or sensory evidence once it is familiar. With the suspension of memory, desire and understanding, the analyst will be exposed to undifferentiated feelings that are usually concealed, as part of the direct experience of psychic reality.

While this is commonly reported in meditative experiences, Bion draws no such parallel. He mentions other attentive practices, apart from this total suspension:

> There is the possibility of suppressing one or all of these functions of memory, desire, understanding, and sense either

together or in turn. Practice in suppression of these faculties may lead to an ability to suppress one or other according to need, so that suspension of one might enhance the effect of domination by the other in a manner analogous to the use of alternate eyes.

(Bion 1970: 44)

However, he is consistent in championing an intuited reality that is quite independent of sense impressions and the thinking he believes they feed:

I would say that the more 'real' the psycho-analyst is the more he can be at one with the reality of the patient. Conversely, the more he depends on actual events the more he relies on thinking that depends on a background of sense impression.

(Bion 1970: 28)

How compatible Bion's clinical philosophy is with a Buddhist framework is a big and underexplored question. There is much in his understanding of thinking as secondary to 'preconceptions' and desires that is compatible with the theories of cognition discussed in Chapter 1. However, in his metapsychology, Bion also remains committed to confessedly mystical conceptions of truth, and something like a soul, that carry the imprint of Vedanta rather than Buddhism.

The strictures of Freud and Bion were intended to sharpen the analysts' receptivity and acuity of observation, including the uncomprehending apprehension of features that would otherwise be obliterated by the usual habits of the analyst's mind. Attention becomes important because training it helps the analyst to observe and to analyse more effectively. However, Bion also acknowledged its direct importance for the analyst's patient:

If the psycho-analyst has not deliberately divested himself of memory and desire the patient can 'feel' this and is dominated by the 'feeling' that he is possessed by and contained in the analyst's state of mind, namely, the state represented by the term 'desire'.

(Bion 1970: 42)

While Bion was still formulating his views on psychoanalytic procedure, Karen Horney had made attention the cornerstone of the analyst's technique. In stating this, she conjoins understanding and attention:

> I have dwelt on the quality of the analyst's attention and understanding because all the help he can give the patient follows from his understanding. Allowing for some exaggeration, analysts would need no books on analytical technique if their understanding was complete.
>
> (Horney 1951: 99)

Horney insisted that effective therapeutic work reflected the quality of the analyst's attention, which should have three (overlapping) qualities: wholeheartedness, comprehensiveness, and productiveness.

By wholeheartedness, Horney says she is referring to the power of concentration or absorption in one's work, with any tendency to be distracted being noted and filed for future reference. She comments that being wholeheartedly in the service of the patient requires a kind of self-forgetting at the same time.

> Another aspect of wholehearted attention is unlimited receptivity . . . letting everything sink in. . . . This kind of concentration of which I am speaking involves your feelings and is not just cold detached observation. Unlimited receptivity means being in it with all your feelings. [Horney is referring particularly to feelings toward patients here.] . . . The best advice I can give is that everything come up, emerge, and at the proper time, be observed.
>
> (Horney 1987: 20–1)

On comprehensiveness, Horney says, 'The meaning of letting all sink in can only be DON'T SELECT TOO EARLY' (21). She describes a number of practical problems with this, including a personal blindness preventing receptivity; interrupting too early (because preconceived ideas impair listening and prevent things from sinking in in a wholehearted way). Horney recommends that analysts need to pay attention to themselves because they are the tool that pays attention to what is going on. Thus, analysts monitor their own attention for signs of interest and disinterest. This is complemented by appreciation of the degree of effort the patient exerts from moment to moment. Throughout, an analyst also pays constant attention to the patient's disturbances and the changes that take place in them. Horney admits that the range is enormous but comments that, as in driving a vehicle, 'The more one understands, the more the observations and impressions fall into line, and the easier it becomes to pay attention to them' (26–7).

The third aspect, productivity, is perhaps the most original. It is also the most problematic, in that Horney gives two quite different accounts of it. Both reflect a (valued) tendency for trained attention to 'set something going' (Horney 1951: 189). In one account (Horney 1987), she describes productivity in terms of the analyst's capacity to make sense of things. In the other (Horney 1951), the productivity of attention is evident in patients' awareness of themselves, their trust in the analyst, their fear of their conflicts, and their acceptance of responsibility for themselves.

It may be no accident that Horney had some personal contact with Zen Buddhism at the time of formulating how, in addition to helping the analyst function as a trained observer, the extension of attention toward the patient might be therapeutic in itself. It may also be worth observing that, once he saw intuition as an end in itself, Bion became highly sceptical of equations between psychoanalysis and 'treatment', and about the value of 'improvement' (cf. Symington and Symington 1996: 171) in a manner incompatible with Horney's faith in measured progress.

Two other analytic writers who successfully integrated Buddhist understanding in their work have provided clarifications about 'bare attention'. Mark Epstein writes, 'It is *the* fundamental tenet of Buddhist psychology that this kind of attention is, in itself, healing' (Epstein 1996: 110). And, after affirming the centrality of attention to every aspect of an analyst's work, Nina Coltart applies the recognition of the healing potential of bare attention directly to psychoanalysis:

> The teaching of Buddhism is what is called *bhavana* or the cultivation of the mind with the direct aim of the relief of suffering in all its forms, however small; the method and the aim are regarded as indissolubly interconnected; so it seems to me logical that neutral attention to the immediate present, which includes first and foremost the study of our own minds,

should turn out to be our sharpest and most reliable therapeutic tool in psychoanalytic technique since there, too, we aim
to study the workings of the mind, our own and others, with a
view to relieving suffering.

(Coltart 1992: 183)

As regards my own practice, and how Buddhism has affected
my clinical work with patients, one of the earliest things I
noticed was the deepening of attention. Bare attention has a sort
of purity about it. It's not a cluttered concept. It's that you
simply become better, as any good analyst knows, at concentrating more and more directly, more purely, on what's going on
in a session. You come to concentrate more and more fully on
this person who is with you here and now, and on what it is they
experience with you; to the point that many sessions become
similar to meditations. When this happens, I usually don't say
very much, but a very, very closely attending to the patient, with
my thought processes in suspension, moving toward what Bion
called 'O'; a state which I see as being 'unthought-out', involving
a quality of intuitive apperception of another person's evolving
truth. All this undoubtedly became easier to do as a result of my
Buddhist practice. Sessions became more frequently like meditations. That is about the most powerful effect Buddhism had
on my clinical practice.

(Coltart 1998: 176–7)

The idea that mindfulness augments processes intrinsic to analytic
procedure includes awareness of the analyst's own reactions as well
as observation of the patient:

If you've done a lot of vipassana and have managed to foster
this split attitude of observation detached from thinking and
reacting, yes, it's got to help the countertransference as well,
hasn't it?

(Coltart 1998: 178)

These two writers illustrate quite different ways of introducing
mindful awareness to psychoanalytic psychotherapy. Coltart did
nothing overtly to change the rules of analytic procedure with her
patients. As the above quotations show, she recognised that the
quality of her own close attention affected the atmosphere and

activity of her sessions, without her needing to change her basic psychoanalytic technique.

Mark Epstein has written even more extensively about the impact of interleaving Buddhist studies with psychotherapeutic training and practice, which, for him, has been significantly different. Epstein has long incorporated psychoanalytic thinking, particularly that of Winnicott, in his psychotherapeutic work, which he refers to as Buddhist psychotherapy, but he has developed a distinctive, eclectic style. In his first book, Epstein suggests that mindfulness training could help other therapists to find the personal resources that Freud had demonstrated in his capacity to work in the intensity of the transference with whatever patients projected there, but which Epstein felt other therapists usually lacked (Epstein 1996: 183–4).

Subsequently, Epstein has advocated a more eclectic stance, likening the role he often adopts with patients to that of a coach who teaches people how to venture into their unexperienced and feared feelings (Epstein 1999: 21). The methods he adopts differ from patient to patient, and can include instructing them in meditation or telling Buddhist stories. While agreeing with therapists from the psychodynamic tradition concerning what people seeking therapy are likely to need, Epstein has gone on to reshape the repertoire of professional responses more radically than Horney.

In general, it appears that mindfulness can be assimilated within psychodynamic therapy at many levels, short of creating a completely new brand of therapy. This reflects the way in which the refinement of attention has been core to psychodynamic practice since its inception and the fact that psychodynamic approaches are identified by their methods rather than by a particular problem or patient group. Before we move to consider the impact of mindfulness across cognitive-behavioural psychotherapies, it seems fitting to summarise a training package that shares both of these characteristics, and that has resisted being labelled as a therapy, although it has become increasingly linked with the techniques of cognitive-behaviour therapy as it has been adopted within mental health settings.

Mindfulness-based stress reduction (MBSR)

The work of Jon Kabat-Zinn (1990) has effectively made personal training in mindfulness available to large numbers of people, without their having to seek it either in the form of spiritual aid or as psychotherapeutic treatment. Something of the spirit of the US Founding Fathers seems to inform the wish to make mindfulness available without any requirement to accept or reject particular religious beliefs, nor to compromise or deny each individual's continuing responsibility for their own health. Mindfulness-based stress reduction (MBSR) grew up as an optional adjunct to standard medical treatments for people attending general hospitals who suffered from painful, disabling, chronic and/or life-threatening illnesses. MBSR training has usually commenced without their being asked to see themselves as psychologically or emotionally impaired. After sampling some introductory exercises in mindfulness, they have had to choose whether to attend a full 8-week, part-time training programme.

Those who do so are then helped to become more mindful in their attitudes to their condition, and in their lives generally, through the programme's core components. These include general education about factors inducing and maintaining stress; use of self-monitoring exercises to become familiar with personal stressors and the impact of feelings and thoughts on stress; training in mindfulness by the use of formal mediations (including yoga), as well as practice at being mindful during everyday activities; and the regular use of group discussion to promote learning of all of these. Each week, new techniques are introduced in a graded sequence, with an expectation that at least one of these will be practised daily for at least 30 minutes. The meditative techniques that are used have been chosen to build up a capacity to direct attention from one object to another, and to give students an opportunity to observe and compare the effects of different procedures in order to make future choices about which procedures are likely to be most helpful to them. The extended exercise likely to be used most frequently through the programme sessions is the 'body scan', a modified version of a vipassana exercise in which attention is moved around the body. Sitting meditations develop the capacity to be mindfully aware of breathing, body sensations and posture before selective attention is paid to sounds, thoughts and emotions in turn. After this, undirected 'choiceless awareness' is practised, to foster a non-clinging openness to whatever experiences arise.

As an illustration, the following instructions for mindful breathing would be consistent with this approach:

Example 1: Sample instructions for mindful breathing (Mace 2007)

1 Settle into a comfortable, balanced, sitting position on a chair or floor in a quiet room.
2 Keep the spine erect. Allow the eyes to close.
3 Bring your awareness to the sensations of contact wherever your body is being supported. Gently explore how this really feels.
4 Become aware of your body's movements during breathing, at the chest and at the abdomen.
5 As the breath passes in and out of the body, bring your awareness to the changing sensations at the abdominal wall. Maintain this awareness throughout each breath and from one breath to the next.
6 Allow the breath simply to breathe, without trying to change or control it, just noticing the sensations that go with every movement.
7 As soon as you notice your mind wandering, bring your awareness gently back to the movement of the abdomen. Do this over and over and over again. Every time, it is fine. It helps the awareness to grow.
8 Be patient with yourself.
9 After 15 minutes or so, bring the awareness gently back to your whole body, sitting in the room.
10 Open the eyes. Be ready for whatever is next.

Mindfulness of the body is also developed through two kinds of movement meditations. In one, sequences of relatively simple and physically undemanding yoga postures are worked through, to provide novel physical sensations as a focus for mindful attention. In the other, 'walking meditation', ordinary walking movements are repeated, at varying speeds, to deepen awareness of the bodily sensations that accompany them. Just as the 'yoga' sequences are a deliberate modification of traditional hatha yoga in detail and in intention, so the other exercises have analogues to classical practices without copying these exactly. The emphasis is on the cultivation of bare attention, whatever the context, whether there is movement or not. So even the walking meditation, superficially closest to its traditional model, is different from it but akin to the other core exercises in MBSR because it omits any commentary about 'now I am doing this . . . now I am doing that . . .'.

The programme can also use techniques whose relation to bare attention is more tangential, although they are likely to improve the quality of meditation. These include visualisation, as when a sense of groundedness and implacability is fostered through picturing and then identifying with a mountain as part of a guided meditation. They also include techniques to foster positive feeling such as loving kindness. These are often introduced when the timetable includes an additional, day-long session three-quarters of the way through the course.

What binds the elements together is a guided education in patterns of personal reactivity, with particular attention being paid to those that are linked to subjective stress. Becoming more sharply aware of the tide of bodily sensations, thoughts and feelings is in the service of greater awareness of their interdependence. Between sessions, students will be encouraged to note down the patterns of their responses to pleasant and unpleasant events and to other people. In the sessions, they will discuss these openly, as practice of the mindfulness exercises supports insight of these kinds. Alongside a broadening awareness of what is going on at any moment, a greater ease and capacity to enjoy, but not be submerged by, individual experiences is usually reported by participants.

The programme's widespread popularity has been underpinned by research evidence of its contribution to the relief of symptoms and suffering across conditions ranging from chronic pain to psoriasis (for reviews, see Bishop 2002; Baer 2003; Grossman et al. 2004). This has included evidence of MBSR's impact on hormones mediating stress responses (Marcus et al. 2003) and immune reactivity (Davidson et al. 2003). Throughout, the effect of MBSR programmes on patients' levels of anxiety and depression has been a consistent theme (Kabat-Zinn et al. 1992; Reibel et al. 2001). Its impacts on psychological health are considered in more detail in the next chapter. Even if the practice of MBSR, as a training that is offered by instructors rather than therapists, has remained substantially unchanged over the last 15 years, it has been the progenitor of a growing range of purpose-built adaptations for specific client groups. These tend to combine some of the core exercises, such as the body scan and sitting meditations, with alternative psychoeducational content and additional stratagems. The willingness to design new therapeutic packages targeted at a defined clinical need, often organised around a plausible theory of symptom formation, has been a characteristic of the cognitive-behavioural tradition that has probably been crucial in gaining such wide acceptance for its methods.

Cognitive-behavioural therapies (CBT)

Quite distinct ways of incorporating mindfulness within psychotherapy have arisen within the cognitive-behavioural tradition over the last 15 years. Cognitive psychology and Buddhist psychology are in broad agreement about the dependence of emotional disturbance on pervasive patterns of thinking and perception. In contrast to most psychodynamic therapies, recent cognitive-behavioural treatments tend to be designed as interventions for people with a specific set of clinical needs or disorder, rather than as a broad-spectrum therapy. These aims have informed the design of a positive flood of new 'mindfulness-based' interventions, which include:

- mindfulness-based cognitive therapy (MBCT)
  (Segal *et al.* 2002)
- mindfulness-based eating awareness training (MB–EAT)
  (Kristeller and Hallett 1999)
- mindfulness-based relapse prevention (MBRP)
  (Witkiewitz *et al.* 2005)
- mindfulness-based relationship enhancement (MBRE)
  (Carson *et al.* 2004)
- dialectical behaviour therapy (DBT)
  (Linehan 1993a)
- acceptance and commitment therapy (ACT)
  (Hayes *et al.* 1999)

Mindfulness-based cognitive therapy (MBCT)

The clinical approach of MBCT's founders was already becoming distinctive within cognitive therapy. Zindel Segal's collaboration with the psychoanalyst Jeremy Safran on interpersonal schemas was a clear demonstration of how relational factors were being brought into the centre of therapy (Safran and Segal 1990). Their recognition of the therapeutic usefulness of 'decentering' from cognitions – rather than trying to remove or change them – was also complemented nicely by John Teasdale's by then long-standing interest in 'differential activation'. This was a way of short-circuiting attention given to negative cognitions, which would otherwise compound the lowering of someone's mood. With Mark Williams, they all shared a theoretical as well as practical interest in the factors that make people vulnerable to repeated depression and the prevention of relapse. Having agreed that a therapeutic strategy based on attentional switching was the way forward, they have been candid about the circumstances that led them to include a far more thorough programme of mindfulness practice within their therapeutic package than they had first thought necessary (cf. Segal *et al.* 2002: 55–7).

As its name suggests, MBCT adds training in specific cognitive skills to the framework of MBSR (Segal *et al.* 2002). MBCT is very similar in its organisation and content to MBSR, although it is usually taught in smaller groups than the 30 or so that have been common in some centres. It also remains similar in ethos, with an expectation that MBCT therapists will have (and maintain) personal experience of mindfulness that they regularly draw on as they assist their patients going through the programme. In comparison, MBCT training in mindfulness has placed marginally less emphasis on bodily movement and has incorporated a 3-minute 'breathing space'. (This is a very brief, transportable routine for rapidly restoring a mindful attitude in three, minute-long, phases: a deliberate review of current events and reactions, becoming mindful of the breath as a means of restoring an internal sense of calm, and a movement back out to the surroundings in which the sense of calm is maintained and carried forward.) Instead of stress education, exercises for the monitoring and analysis of dysfunctional thinking and its specific relationship to body sensations and mood are included. Yet, in essentials, very little is changed – the decentering from negative cognitions that is overtly worked toward in MBCT being equivalent to the mindfulness of thinking that MBSR has always aimed to teach. Although MBCT was originally developed as a prophylactic intervention for use with people with an established history of relapsing depression, it is being increasingly used as a treatment intervention in its own right. Variants have developed to meet the specific needs of other client groups with mental health problems, which take into account the particular difficulties they face from a cognitive perspective, as well as particular needs they may have in engaging with the treatment approach.

For instance, mindfulness-based eating awareness training (MB–EAT) represents an extension of MBSR and MBCT designed for people with binge eating disorder. The resulting programme is usually longer than 8 weeks, and is premised upon mindfulness practice reversing the lack of awareness of bodily and internal states that has been commonly observed among people with eating disorders. In practice, Kristeller and Hallett have found restoration of sensitivity to feelings of satiety to be therapeutically essential. A complementary goal with this population has been to provide a means of living with prominent guilt feelings. Meditations designed to foster feelings of forgiveness are a key component of the programme for this reason. (Here modern practice is replicating traditional Buddhist training, where meditations to develop concentration and mindfulness are often interspersed with others that develop positive social emotions such as loving kindness or compassion.) At the same time, as the name suggests, MB–EAT has placed particular emphasis on the practice of mindfulness in the kitchen rather than in meditation sessions to ensure it is employed where it is needed most. As the list of interventions indicates, other variants of MBCT and MBSR have been derived to meet other clinical needs. They are discussed further in the next chapter.

In moving from MBSR to MBCT, mindfulness interventions have become more like other therapies, with the instructor likely to be seen as a therapist. Other adaptations have also been made in response to the perceived needs of people diagnosed with mental disorders, a major example being the distinctive framework devised for dialectical behaviour therapy.

Dialectical behaviour therapy (DBT)

For many mental health professionals, DBT is the only therapy drawing on mindfulness that they can name. It is a relatively complex treatment with a complex philosophy. As its name suggests, its goal was originally a behavioural one, reducing self-harming behaviour in the form of taking overdoses, self-cutting or deliberately seeking dangerous situations. Intended for people with a repeated history of such acts, it was also fostered as a treatment for borderline personality disorder (BPD), in which such behaviour is especially common (and one of the criteria for the diagnosis).

Although some elements of the design of DBT can appear less necessary and harder to transmit than others (not least the concept of 'dialectics'), it is a package of therapeutic techniques and teachings that reflects a distinct perception of the origins of the psychological difficulties common to people diagnosed with BPD, and an analysis of the limitations of alternative treatments. In fact, a direct link is made between these two – people with BPD, having repeatedly faced experiences of invalidation in their early as well as their adult lives, are especially prone to experience further rejection of themselves during conventional psychological treatments. Linehan sees this risk in CBT's traditional emphasis on targets and change. This is at the expense of acceptance, which DBT therapists are expected to demonstrate and to help their clients find for themselves. The continuing importance of striking a creative and acceptable balance between acceptance and change is one justification for the therapy's being 'dialectical'. The philosophy of acceptance permeates the model of BPD that underpins treatment. The pathology results from multiple 'dysregulations' – of mood, interpersonal relationships, sense of self, behaviour and cognition. In each case, there has been a vicious cycle of nature and nurture that, without any imputation of failure, compromises the adult's moves to maintain control. Instead, there are extremes and discontinuities that, in the case of emotional dysregulation, for instance, are likely to reflect lasting changes in the way the brain processes experiences and affords responses to them. As a first step toward self-acceptance, patient and therapist need to agree on an accurate picture of this dysregulation, its likely origins and continuing consequences, without these becoming a source of further recrimination.

DBT was created as a mindfulness-based, but not a meditation-based, therapy. There is a formal split in its structure between therapeutic sessions, provided through individual meetings with a personal therapist, and skills training, provided in a group format alongside other people with BPD. The skills learned are divided into acceptance skills (in the form of mindfulness and distress tolerance) and change skills (regulation of emotions and interpersonal effectiveness). However, mindfulness skills are clearly first among apparent equals. They are taught first, and constantly referred back to in the presentation of other skill types. This teaching takes place in a didactic group setting, in which members of the therapist team provide lectures and seminars, whose learning points are reinforced through group discussion of their relevance to patients' own experiences and predicaments and the provision of printed handouts for further study. The first element to be presented is perhaps Linehan's most significant contribution to the study of 'mindfulness'. It is a delineation between three forms of 'mind', termed 'reasonable mind', 'emotional mind' and 'wise mind'.

To understand what is most characteristic of Linehan's model of the divided mind, it can be helpful to compare it with two famous tripartite mental models that preceded it (and seem to inform it) – those of Plato and Freud. What all three have in common is a recognition of the scope for conflict between aspects of the mind, based upon their capacity to influence its actions. Plato distinguished appetitive, passionate and rational aspects. Although these are difficult to translate exactly into modern psychology, their potential for conflict is graphically illustrated in his metaphor of the chariot, in which the horses of desire and passion strain against the efforts of the charioteer, reason, to tame them (cf. Plato's *Phaedrus*). In the Freudian model of id, ego and superego (Freud 1923), appetite and reason continue to characterise the first two, embodying the concepts of the pleasure principle and the reality principle. While their opposition is sustained through divisions drawn between what is unconscious and conscious, the superego defies this functional distinction by including unconscious affects, such as guilt, as well as conscious ideals that inform a person's ideas about what they should strive to be like. According to this model, conflict is manifest not only in the pull of instinctual wishes, but also from opposition experienced in the ego in its relation to the shoulds of the superego.

In comparison, divisions within Linehan's model are functional rather than structural. In a way that is very consistent with the Platonic model, the different modes of mind can each be experienced as being in control at different times, and they can rapidly displace one another. The relationship between the wise mind and the rational mind can resemble healthy assertion of the ego against the strict demands of the superego in the Freudian model. According to Linehan, when logical thinking dictates intentions, the rational mind is in play; when strong feelings dictate, the emotional mind is in control, and the content of thoughts will reflect this. The wise mind transcends both of these, being recognised only when reason and feeling are in balance. In addition, intuition will be engaged, and there will be a sense of cohesion underlying conscious experience. The mindfulness skills instructor therefore works initially to help clients discriminate between these modes of functioning, and to reject the results of emotional mind acting in isolation.

Linehan's description of individual mindfulness skills emanates from a model aimed to serve the needs of people experiencing considerable internal chaos and for whom clear structures and guidance are likely to be welcome. Indeed, she offers what is effectively a cognitive-behavioural analysis of them. Three 'what' skills are complemented by three 'how' skills. The former comprise observing, description and spontaneous participation. These activities are seen as mutually incompatible and are to be practised separately. Observation involves stepping back to ensure that a mindful awareness is engaged. It is intended to be the antithesis of the impulsivity to which people with BPD are ordinarily prone. Description, involving the deliberate naming of events as they occur, is seen as an important step in discriminating between incorrect construction of situations and a more objective perspective. Spontaneity in action may appear to risk confusion with impulsivity, but the goal is a wholehearted commitment to mindful action that is free from conflict. The three 'how' skills apply to all of these 'whats'. They concern being non-judgemental, one-minded and effective. These counteract, respectively, the client group's tendency to adopt highly polarised opinions (whether idealising or harshly critical), to succumb to mindlessness or distraction, and to be so influenced by assumptions concerning other people's reactions or rigid principles that they fail to meet the needs of the moment in order to propitiate a private form of pride. After these skills are practised through a series of exercises, they are brought to bear on the subjects of the remaining three modules, that is, emotions, distressing experience and relationships.

If the emphasis on awareness is common to other mindfulness-based approaches, Linehan's approach shows the influence of Zen most in its emphasis on spontaneous action as a goal (among the 'what' skills) and in its view of the therapist's role. Zen teaching, characteristically iconoclastic and antitheoretical, has always held complete identification between thought and action as an ideal. The means it has adopted to induce such a state of being, particularly in the Rinzai Zen tradition, has included unexpected and paradoxical interventions from a Zen teacher designed to nudge the student into the fundamentally different state of being ('enlightenment') that is the goal of Zen study. This can range from the

setting of cryptic questions ('koans') for the student to contemplate, to provocative demonstrations. Linehan's therapists are
encouraged to see their task as assisting patients in the discovery of
their own 'wise mind' in a way that presumes they have some
greater understanding of this, and to adopt an 'irreverent' attitude
that has the power to provoke and surprise. When working
individually with clients, the therapist also has considerable licence
to intervene in order to guide them toward responses likely to be in
tune with the 'wise mind'.

To act in this way naturally requires a complementary set of
skills from the therapist. However, these, too, are learned on the
basis of a behavioural analysis of the role, rather than a personal
internalisation of attitudes, awareness and non-reactivity. DBT
therapists rarely undergo DBT themselves. Moreover, as teachers
of mindfulness, they are free to decide how they should experience
it for themselves. The implications of such differences in approach
are discussed more fully below.

Lynch and colleagues (2006), recognising how a Zennish form of
mindfulness will emphasise being completely immersed in action,
suggest four mechanisms for the effectiveness of mindfulness within
DBT. These are 1. behavioural exposure and learning new responses
(such as non-doing); 2. emotion regulation (by decoupling negative
response and amplifying cognitive appraisals); 3. reducing belief
in internal rules (which tend to feed undermining self-images); and
4. attentional control. By the last, they are referring to a learned
capacity to focus on process at will, rather than the objects of
attention. However, some therapists appear to interpret this as
teaching a capacity to divert attention at will to other, more
benign, objects through distraction rather than a change of attentional mode.

While it is potentially helpful to try to analyse the mode of action
in this way, the analysis offered by Lynch *et al.* (2006) is unlikely to
be the last word. Strictly speaking, it lists effects of mindfulness in
terms of changes secondary to other processes, rather than mechanisms by which mindfulness has such effects. (The point will
become clearer in the discussion below of Martin's work.) The
importance of being as specific as possible about the mechanisms
through which mindfulness works is evident from the discrepancy
between different accounts of how mindfulness acts within DBT.
For instance, reduction in impulsive behaviours during DBT has
been attributed both to an improved capacity to participate with

awareness in all the processes that lead up to an action (e.g. Linehan 1993b: 63), and to greater acceptance of the painful negative emotions that otherwise trigger impulsive actions (e.g. Welch *et al.* 2006: 122). Before making the explanations fit theoretical abstractions such as 'affect regulation', it may be important to ground them in successful clients' own accounts of how their functioning has changed.

Acceptance and commitment therapy (ACT)

Like MBCT and DBT, acceptance and commitment therapy (often called 'act' rather than ACT for short) has been named as a 'third-wave' cognitive therapy. It is based on a radical behavioural analysis of patients' difficulties. From this, a selection of appropriate therapeutic stratagems is made from a full and varied menu. They fall under six main headings, four of which are acknowledged to be 'mindfulness functions', that is, 'contact with the present moment', 'acceptance', 'cognitive defusion', and 'self as context'. The first two correspond to the receptive awareness and to the suspension of judgement that have been key to modern conceptions of mindfulness. The third, 'cognitive defusion', a deliberate disidentification from thoughts, is the expected outcome of a series of exercises that focus directly on clients' relationship to their thoughts. An example of the kind of practical exercise that a therapist might introduce for this follows. In practice, it would be followed by detailed examination of the client's experience by the therapist to underline the intended lesson.

Example 2: Specimen ACT exercise to facilitate cognitive defusion (after Mace 2007)

This exercise is to help you see the difference between looking at your thoughts and looking from your thoughts. Imagine you are on the bank of a steadily flowing stream, looking down at the water. Upstream, some trees are dropping leaves which are floating past you on the surface of the water. Just watch them passing by, without interrupting the flow. Whenever you are aware of a thought, let the words be written on one of the leaves as it carries on floating by. Allow the leaf to carry the thought away. If a thought is more of a picture thought, let a leaf take on the image as it moves along. If you get thoughts about the exercise, see these, too, on a leaf. Let them be carried away like any other thought, as you carry on watching.

At some point, the flow will seem to stop. You are no longer on the bank seeing the thoughts on the leaves. As soon as you notice this, see if you can catch what was happening just before the flow stopped. There will be a thought that you have 'bought'. See how it took over. Notice the difference between thoughts passing by and thoughts thinking for you. Do this whenever you notice the flow has stopped. Then return to the bank, letting every thought find its leaf as it floats steadily past.

The fourth function, 'self as context', is characteristic of ACT, referring to a perspectival shift in which the client is encouraged to check and reject assumptions about the substantiality and continuity of the experienced self. ACT aims to be flexibly adapted to a wide range of clinical problems (and therapist preferences). Because its exercises are often elaborate, yet intended to be adapted to several situations, they do not always fit easily into the formal/ informal framework that is introduced in Chapter 5 of this book. If the repertoire of existing exercises does not match a particular clinical need, or a client's preferences, the therapist is encouraged to devise one. Throughout, means are adjusted to goals. There is no requirement for therapist or patient to undergo formal meditation as a means to any of the mindfulness functions, although they are free to choose to.

As a radical behavioural intervention, ACT resembles psychodynamic therapies rather than cognitive therapies in much of its practice, because it tailors its approach to the individual at the level of personal formulation, rather than having methods that are specific to diagnosed disorders. (ACT also has much in common with existential and psychodynamic therapies in the components which are not discussed here – its attention to clients' underlying values.)

Apart from contrasts in their procedures, all of the CBT-based interventions discussed in this section differ in their tone from those psychodynamic treatments that incorporate mindfulness. Branded with catchy multiletter acronyms that could equally belong to pharmaceutical magic bullets, they tend to be described in the language of treatment. They can therefore present a paradox in the way they promote attitudes of acceptance and 'letting go' alongside a relatively prescriptive and active therapeutic style. Some unavoidable tension between formed intentions to be mindful and non-doing was noted in Chapter 1, and is familiar to meditation teachers of all persuasions. Within therapeutic contexts, the contradiction is not without practical consequences, some of which are discussed elsewhere (Mace, in press). We have seen that meditation itself can take a back seat in some of these structured approaches, making it important to confirm, through formal process studies as well as qualitative reports, that their effects are being mediated by real changes in the capacity to be mindfully aware.

Mindfulness as a group intervention

While we have been considering mindfulness therapies in relation to the traditional categories of individual psychotherapy, it is important to remember that those in which the emphasis on mindfulness is most explicit are essentially group interventions. How, then, do these compare with more traditional forms of group psychotherapy? They are unique in a number of respects. Some years ago, I proposed a simple ABC method of delineating the differences between one group approach and another that was not dependent on theory (Mace 2002). It may be useful here. Three parameters are used to codify how a group works: its approach to affect in the group, the handling of boundaries, and the communicational style that a particular model fosters. It turns out that mindfulness-based group interventions can not only be collectively differentiated from formal therapeutic groups on each of these dimensions, but they also serve to highlight differences between, say, MBSR and DBT groups.

The attitude to affect in mindfulness groups is to turn the attention inward toward it, to face it, to recognise all the ways in which it presents, including somatic manifestations, and not to inhibit its expression as emotion. Particular techniques might be introduced for coping with particularly painful affect, such as sharing awareness with the breath when instructions might be given to 'breathe through it', but these are likely to serve to increase mindfulness of the affect, rather than avoidance of it. It is not necessary to try to narrate the affect, to integrate it within a story either of where it seems to belong in someone's past experience, or of how it might reflect experiences in the group itself. Two secondary aspects of the handling of affect reflect stylistic differences between mindful therapies. One is the deliberate attention to affect with a view to developing a future capacity to tolerate it, as in the teaching of mindful 'distress tolerance skills' within DBT. The other is the deliberate cultivation of positive affects through meditative inner focusing. The commonest example is probably the use of 'loving kindness' meditations to develop and become more open to loving feelings toward others. Originally, a component of retreat days held toward the end of MBSR courses, these meditations appear to be becoming increasingly popular. The use of forgiveness meditations within MB–EAT is another example of the fostering of positive affect.

Turning to boundaries, mindfulness groups are closer to time-extended psychoeducational groups than any other in their structure. They cater for relatively large numbers of clients, and alternate between overt teaching, group discussion, and guided exercises. Boundary management by the leader is likely to need to be flexible and skilful; for instance, leaders should have the facility not to be totally ruled by a session-by-session plan, so that a sequence of skills training can unfold in a way and at a pace that best meets the needs of the individual participants. There is likely to be clear phasing of sessions, with an initial review of experiences since the previous meeting, and a final pulling together of material covered with explicit instructions for practices to be undertaken prior to the next session. Within a session, boundary management can involve division of the group into smaller units, for instance, for joint exercises in which non-visual sensation is explored, or for the discussion of potentially sensitive material.

Communication within mindfulness groups is very varied. Interaction through touch as well as verbal communication may be invited between members at some points. Group discussions are likely to involve members building upon others' comments in the exploration of a theme rather than in personal analysis. Session leaders have to be able to communicate in many ways. They provide some overt scene setting and teaching about the approach. They lead discussions in which their role is to respond to and validate contributions, without trying either to make these into something else through interpretation or to provide further guidance in a way that denies participants' own expertise or fore-closes options for them. The leaders also provide direct instruction in mindfulness techniques. We have already seen some of the different forms these take (pp. 59–68). The various formats do involve different modes of communication. Helping people to apply effectively instructions of the kind cited in example 1 calls on different aptitudes than leading an exercise based on example 2. The former will involve more demonstration as well as instruction, with learning occurring through imitation as well as comprehension. This means that communication is through not only how things are said, as well as what is said, but also how the conductor behaves in other respects. The MBSR and MBCT tradition in particular has emphasised the importance of instructors embodying in their presentation the thing they are trying to teach.

Integrating mindfulness within psychotherapeutic practice

Treatments like MBCT, DBT and ACT are integrated treatments in the sense that they have been recently created as a complete therapeutic package, in which mindfulness has a relatively clear relationship to the other components within the package. They have been manualised to assist formal evaluation, and it is possible to undertake a formal assessment of a therapist's 'adherence' to the approved model. However, there are other senses by which mindfulness can be integrated within psychotherapeutic practice. A flexible and eclectic approach that would be much harder for other therapists to emulate is seen in Mark Epstein's 'Buddhist psychotherapy' discussed earlier in this chapter. Other therapies may incorporate mindfulness as a result of the therapist's attitude in the course of the treatment, or of the patient practising mindfulness for some or all of the treatment period, with nothing being visibly different from other treatments of the same type.

These can seem very obvious ways for therapists to introduce mindfulness into their work. One of the perennial hazards of such practices is that they are very difficult to evaluate, as it is so much harder to demonstrate equivalence between what several therapists or several patients are doing privately alongside the treatment. It is interesting therefore that one of the earliest studies of mindfulness in psychotherapy (Kutz et al. 1985b) was a study of 20 patients who attended a 10-week programme that included mindfulness of breathing, body and movement, while they continued working in long-term psychotherapy. The non-meditating therapists assessed the impact of this on the participants' clinical status, and on their capacity to use the psychotherapy. There were small changes on some clinical parameters, reflecting an overall reduction of negativity and anxiety, although hostility, relationships, family and sexual adjustment, and emotional inhibition were apparently unaffected. However, several of these patients and their therapists noted mutative experiences in the course of meditation, some involving a capacity to access feelings and memories that had been untouched for years despite their intervention, together with improvements in insight and capacity to use the therapy productively thereafter.

While this is a more mundane approach than innovatory packages, and less specific in its impact because the patients were already in treatment for a range of difficulties, it is of huge potential importance. If augmentation of therapeutic effects through a relatively brief and inexpensive intervention like this mindfulness training package is as significant and consistent as it appeared to be from Kutz's study, they could be translated into real improvements in cost efficiency (Kutz et al. 1985a). They would also be relatively simple to incorporate within public sector psychotherapy services, which are often responsible for providing treatments for more than 100 people simultaneously.

Despite this, the only apparent attempt to replicate or extend the study has been a smaller, albeit controlled, one in which patients attending an MBSR course early in therapy were compared to controls who were receiving comparable treatment but no MBSR (Weiss et al. 2005). Although there was little immediate impact on clinical status, those receiving MBSR were reported to have higher scores on a measure of goal achievement specific to the study. Most significantly, they went on to terminate their therapies sooner than members of the control group, pressing the economic argument home for further serious consideration of joint provision of mindfulness training alongside exploratory psychotherapy.

Implications of mindfulness-based interventions for psychotherapy

By concentrating on treatments that have either highlighted the role of attention or are the most likely to be provided within a public mental health service, this survey is far from exhaustive. There are other approaches having strong affinities to the humanistic or person-centred traditions where mindfulness has been incorporated, not simply because it usefully extends the therapist's tool kit, but also because the therapeutic work explicitly adopts goals that overlap with those of traditional spiritual pursuits. This is evidently so with the contemplative (e.g. Wellings and McCormick 2006) and transpersonal therapies (Rowan 2005) as well as the explicitly Buddhist psychotherapy for which David and Caroline Brazier have devised a formal training programme (Brazier 2003). This convergence of goals will be discussed further when underlying aims of therapy are reconsidered in Chapter 6.

The variety of ways that mindfulness can be intentionally offered as a helping intervention outside a traditional Buddhist framework that have been examined here still represent a considerable range. They differ not only in their methods but also in their aims. Psychodynamic and many of the mindfulness-based treatments are open to use across many conditions: others are highly specific. These therapies can differ, too, in what is actually known about how far their effects are consonant with their stated aims (a topic taken up in Chapter 4).

All of these contrasts are relevant to the different ways that the trainer or therapist is expected to work. The accounts already given highlight differences in the level of overt activity that is expected, and in how far this should be explanatory, educational, group focused and so forth. Beyond these, there are critical differences in the expected relationship of the therapist to mindfulness. As already noted in the discussion of group leadership, there has been a strong insistence within MBSR on the teacher's ability not only to experience mindfulness at first hand in order to develop it in others, but also to embody it as a living demonstration that students would internalise. Conversely, those approaches that place less emphasis on guided meditations, including DBT and ACT, tend to emphasise the importance of the non-meditative tools they promote and to downplay the significance of the therapist's personal experience. These vacillations are hardly new, being mirrored in debates about the role of therapists' personal preparation that have continued to divide the psychoanalytic and cognitive-behavioural traditions within traditional psychotherapies.

The differences between Buddhist psychology and the theoretical frameworks underpinning the principal psychotherapeutic approaches remain considerable, despite apparent similarities. The Buddhist view of mind understands all thought, not only that prone to clear emotional bias, to be projective and inherently distorting reality. However, it goes beyond this, in seeing distortions (whose character varies from mind to mind) at more subtle levels of preconception, and even in the form that consciousness takes. Psychodynamic thinking also has a primary concern with the mediation of experience through human relationships. Although this is relatively underplayed in most Western accounts of it, Buddhist psychology is keenly aware of the relational nature of all processes (psychological, human and otherwise), pointing to a radically relational reality in which the transience of everything is immediately apparent. At the same time, psychodynamic thinking is concerned to understand and develop, but, nevertheless, to maintain, the sense of self. Buddhist psychology, linking suffering and delusion so inextricably to the individualist 'I', admits no real compromise away from the sense that this 'I' is, at its heart, illusory. Psychodynamic thinkers who engage with Buddhism therefore are sometimes left to struggle to produce compromises concerning the self whose intricacy might be worthy of a medieval scholastic, but which evidence the depth of this difficulty (cf. Safran 2003).

Psychodynamic thinkers have more difficulty with the question of the self than either cognitive or systemic therapists. The version of the cognitive paradigm that would reduce the mind to an information-processing system would only have a place for a 'self' if its operational advantages were clear – and this appears to be far from the case. Cybernetics have also informed systemic thinking, in which the concept of any personal 'parts' as needing to be constantly reformed in the flux of systemic reorganisation, rather than being some fixed locatable entity, is consistent with its guiding assumptions.

The primacy of thinking for cognitivists is both the strength and the weakness of attempts to integrate it with Buddhist psychology. The apparent capacity of thoughts to prompt feelings, judgements and moods, both consciously and preconsciously, is well recognised. However, the implication that there is a way of thinking that, free from distortion, is a sufficient condition of psychological health is only partly accepted. It is true that 'right thought' (or *sankappa*, often also translated as 'right intention') is one of the steps of the Noble Eightfold Path. Right thought is cultivated by deliberate attention to and questioning of thoughts as they arise.

Those that are found to be unwholesome in their content and likely consequences are to be set aside in favour of those that will promote wholesome attitudes and actions (for an exposition of this, see *sutta* no. 19 in the *Majhima Nikaya*). Such a habit of thinking can assist the establishment of its dominant twin among the factors promoting wisdom, known as 'right understanding' (*ditthi*, or 'right view'). However, right thought, however refined, cannot in itself lead to right understanding, by which is meant a complete realisation of the nature of suffering, such that there is liberation from it. It is common ground to all the major Buddhist traditions that a realisation of this kind is not a conceptual understanding.

In the face of division between the different Western psychotherapies, we might consider how an interest in attention cuts across traditions within psychotherapy that are generally jealous of their differences and that appear to have quite distinct identities. The intersections can be theoretical and practical. Two writers have made interesting suggestions of this kind that deserve reassessment. In an extensive paper, Jeffrey Martin (1997) notes that 'the processes of mindfulness have been tacitly contained in Western psychotherapies all along' (Martin 1997: 292). As a psychotherapy integrationist, he is keen to demonstrate that mindfulness could be a factor common to many therapies whose contribution is to optimise the opportunity for change within a therapy. He believes this took a consistently different form in psychoanalytic and cognitive-behavioural psychotherapies. In elaborating this, he does tend to work from idealised models of either. In writing about mindfulness, he is also heavily influenced by Ellen Langer's cognitive conception, in which mindfulness is identified with the capacity to shift one's mindset easily between multiple perspectives (Langer 1989) rather than Buddhistic ones.

Martin identifies the psychoanalytic position with the 'open-form attention' that is achieved by following Freud's injunction. Most interestingly, he likens the shift in personal perspective that this requires from the analyst with the 'decentering' that Safran and Segal (1990) saw as an important therapeutic objective in cognitive therapy, one whose role was enhanced in MBCT. Martin was sensitive to the ambivalence of how the movement of stepping out of usual perspectives could apply to either therapist or patient, with both needing to set aside a wish for mastery and replace it with what he calls 'fresh awareness'. He sees verbal interpretations of unconscious conflicts or transference as an aspect of this, by shifting a patient's centre of awareness, so that the overall contribution of mindfulness here is 'to help create an interval of time wherein Bill can view his landscape more intentionally rather than simply react'. This is contrasted with what Martin calls 'focused-form attention', seen as necessary for insight to be translated into action.

> The implementation of focused-form attention in the present moment utilizes the insight that was previously acquired within the psychodynamic orientation, and like a catalyst, helps convert it into action through the employment of cognitive-behavioral methodology.
>
> (Martin 1997: 305)

Focused-form attention brings about deautomisation by the interruption of, or disidentification with, automatic sequences. Martin comments, 'Through repeated focusing of mindfulness attention, more adaptive and previously less dominant forms of experience are reinforced' (305).

How valid is this attempt to polarise the two approaches in terms of different attentional strategies? The relationship between insight and action in psychodynamic therapies is a hugely important one, but Martin's cognitivist preoccupations do not let him follow Safran's own views here (Safran 1989). Safran clearly differentiates intellectual insight, which may or may not inform action, from the immediate insight that is often available at a non-verbal somatic level, particularly in transferential situations, that does prompt new forms of action. Martin seems to see focused-form attention as a kind of searchlight that allows an operation to be performed following additional voluntary actions, giving examples that include cognitive restructuring. The thrust of the work of Teasdale, Segal and Williams has been to cast doubt on the effectiveness or the usefulness of operations to replace one set of thoughts by another. By talking instead of 'differential activation' of entire modes of processing (e.g. Teasdale 1999), they have placed 'decentering' centre stage in the operation of cognitive therapeutic approaches. These objections need not detract from the simple identification of broad, evenly receptive awareness with psychodynamic work, and narrow-focused attention with cognitive-behavioural approaches, although Speeth describes how attentional shifts across the full range of breadth of focus occur within ordinary psychotherapeutic work, commenting that the extremes of what she calls 'focused' and 'panoramic' attention 'must be seen as more heuristic than natural categories' (Speeth 1982: 145).

Finally, following Deikman, Segal and others, Martin's invocation of a process of 'deautomisation' as typical of CBT needs careful consideration. His instrumentalist approach suggests that focused attention is a precursor to another operation that will make the difference. The implication is that, in order to change a bad habit, it is necessary first to see things in such a concentrated way that the steps are clear, before deliberately changing the steps. In this sense, the cognitive restructuring that he sees as a key technique is like a musician playing a musical passage very deliberately and slowly in order to change the fingering pattern they use, or a motorist driving very slowly in order to master the actions necessary to drive a car whose steering wheel and instruments are on the opposite side to the one with which they are familiar. In either case, it seems attention has to be accompanied by deliberate, corrective actions. This does not really deal with the possibility that awareness is sufficient in itself for deautomisation – that links within series of actions are not only recognised but are attenuated at the same time by the attentive process. This would represent another way in which mindfulness introduced something that was common across therapeutic processes under different models, but which was really not adequately explained by current paradigms.

Future developments

It is possible that mindful therapy is a reformative development, tapping a therapeutic dimension that is not adequately realised within current maps of the therapeutic landscape. It is also possible that it may prompt some revision of the maps. While it is too early to assess this, some future directions of travel can be sketched. Mindfulness interfaces with three other broad currents in psychotherapeutic thinking and practice, each of which is already challenging the traditional divisions in their own right. These are interest in the brain, interest in the body, and interest in what I prefer to call the transpersonal.

Brain therapy

There is now enormous interest in biological substrates that are potentially associated with the developmental difficulties with which psychotherapists are called upon to work. There has been great interest in the topic of affect regulation, Schore (1994) using it to organise his entire review of evidence for functional hierarchical relationships within the brain. Their great sensitivity to attachment experiences during early development accounts for variations in the capacity to regulate affects in adulthood. Accordingly, the success of therapeutic approaches in later life will depend on how well such failures in early attunement are addressed, a theme elaborated also by Fonagy *et al.* (2002).

While there is no shortage of colourful hypotheses about the biological basis of therapeutic action, *in vivo* investigations of the effects of therapy being provided for people with mental disorders remain rare (Mace 2003). Linehan (1993a) has underlined the potential importance of mindfulness in modulating affect, and this could provide the kind of specific therapeutic effect that is necessary to demonstrate clear correlations with brain processes. Chapter 2 started with a summary of research concerning brain activity associated with mindfulness. As recordings grow in sophistication, it is likely that these efforts will be limited by continuing conceptual confusions concerning the scope of mindfulness, to the point where neurobiology might help to demarcate truly mindful awareness. For instance, this could be a state in which, apart from increased coherence, there is a bilateral increase in the power of alpha and theta as well as fast beta waves relative to the ordinary waking state. This would contrast with other meditative states, in which there is more exclusive enhancement of one of these bands and/or delta activity.

The body

It is clear from both the traditional literature on mindfulness and the experiences of practitioners that mindfulness depends on awareness of our embodiment. Beyond the range of 'mindful' experience, it is rare for accounts of other meditative or 'peak' experiences not to involve distinctive bodily sensations.

Despite Freud's injunction to remember that 'the ego is a body ego' (Freud 1914b), psychotherapy has been quite ambivalent about bodies – whether the patient's or the therapist's own body. Psychoanalysis has been plagued by the perceived need to recoil from and reject any somatic elements in technique – from Freud's decision to stop touching patients and the condemnation, persecution and excommunication as heretics of somatically focused analysts such as Ferenczi and Reich. Even today, psycho-analytic organisations can professionally penalise individuals who show an interest in the bodily contribution to memory and uncon-scious life. This has led to a situation in which therapies with an overt somatic focus have been seen as less than respectable and as requiring a separate professional structure.

Rather than encouraging direct manipulation, some therapies, such as Gendlin's (1996) focusing, have developed techniques for deliberately directing attention toward internal sensations in emotionally charged areas such as the chest and the solar plexus in order to activate feelings and images so that these come more fully into awareness. While he was aware of parallels with medita-tion, Gendlin did not refer directly to mindfulness within this attention-focusing technique. Yet, it has much in common with the kind of mindful therapy techniques that have been reviewed here. There seems to be considerable potential for their combination, not least in the capacity of mindfulness to contain as well as unlock somatically linked experience.

There is also a split between the content of psychotherapeutic training, and therapists' declared attitudes to the body, and the considerable use they make of it in practice in the course of their work (Shaw 2004). This is starting to change as some therapists are becoming more willing to cross professional boundaries, seeing bodily experiences as central to psychotherapeutic work rather than as a dispensable epiphenomenon. Growing interest in mindfulness may help to reorganise the very disparate field of 'body therapies' by discriminating between those that depend upon physical interven-tion and those that do not, but pay very close attention to the body.

The transpersonal

I use the term 'transpersonal' to refer to those aspects of our minds that are not exclusively dedicated to defining and pursuing indi-vidual needs and interests. It seems preferable to 'spiritual' and its variants, none of which seem to come without all kinds of con-notations that are rarely shared. (In any case, talk of soul or spirit seems ill-suited to the agnostic and antiessentialist context in which mindfulness arose.) Whatever term is used, it does seem that an interest in personal transcendence is currently fuelling the greatest resurgence of transpersonal thinking in psychotherapy since Jung.

Buddhist thought and practices have been influential in other ways than the development of mindful therapies, leading to innovations which complement mindful practices. One example is the direct harnessing of the transpersonal affects of the 'perfections' or *brahmaviharas*, as in the meditative cultivation of compassion within compassionate mind training (Gilbert 2005). This is a method of neutralising the toxic self-attacking that can be very prominent in people having a strong sense of shame who are liable to depression. Another practice, aiming to put understanding of no-self or *anatta* into effect, is the development of therapeutic strategies to reduce destructive egotism through recognition of its illusoriness (Leary 2004).

In the field of psychotherapy, while interest in the transcendent functions predates Freud, they, too, have been split off from the time of Jung, attracting a notoriety among the most institutionalised therapies that is reminiscent of the history of somatic therapies. Again, there are contradictions between official attitudes and individual practitioners' actual interest in the transpersonal (cf. Simmonds 2004), meaning that here, too, therapists often seamlessly integrate a transpersonal dimension within their practice without necessarily drawing attention to the fact.

The need for in-depth case studies

Observations such as these may be interesting, but are unlikely to bring about change by themselves. Wherever psychotherapy is headed, it is an arena where progress is ultimately made by the demonstration of a technique's value with real patients, through documented case histories. These reports need to be sufficiently detailed so that the steps are clear, and readers can form their own view on the relationships between process and effects. This has been as true for the major innovations that followed psychoanalysis as for Freud's own example. Mindfulness-based psychotherapy is unlikely to be an exception. It is also true that this basic requirement to provide persuasive case histories is under many threats at present. These range from clinical journals that simply deem all case reports unworthy of their consideration, to editors who take such a zealous attitude to anonymisation that most published reports are automatically fictionalised beyond the point that accurate clinical inferences can be drawn from them, irrespective of the wishes of those they concern.

When it comes to clinical reporting, mindful therapies are faced with a similar paradox to the one facing scientific investigation of mindfulness, outlined in the previous chapter. A thorough examination of mindful psychotherapy requires methods that are appropriate and sensitive to its process. Some crucial clinical questions – for example, how far therapists need to embody mindfulness in order to foster mindfulness in their clients and for this to be therapeutic – have already been identified. Whatever third-party investigations might be set up to resolve them, psychotherapists are likely to seek additional evidence of a different kind. For a case history to illuminate the process of a mindful intervention, it would need to provide in-depth descriptions of a therapist's awareness and of the ways in which it fluctuated, alongside a detailed account of the internal changes experienced by the patient (or patients). This would depend upon unusually detailed, contemporaneous records concerning all parties. The paradox at present is how the few published descriptions of completed therapies using mindfulness have continued to minimise detail and permit only very general inferences. The need for truly comprehensive case reports may be the most immediate challenge for the field to overcome if it is to advance its understanding and engage the interest of greater numbers of psychotherapists.

Conclusions

Mindfulness is integral to well-established forms of psychotherapy, including psychoanalytic psychotherapy, as well as an ingredient in newer interventions that were designed to help patients become more mindful. Mindfulness can therefore be an attitude that is brought to bear on work within an established framework, as well as something that is taught in order to bring about specific desired effects. As overtly mindfulness-based interventions have been used with people with mental health difficulties, they have taken on more of the character of a therapy than an educational or coaching intervention. Perceived limitations in some clients' ability to engage with traditional meditative techniques for developing mindfulness have led to the development of alternative exercises that might be less demanding but which are therapeutically beneficial. Intervention packages have continued to be adapted to address specific mental health problems through the other elements they include alongside some training in mindfulness. The field may be being held back by the relative absence of case reports that allow the dynamics of awareness to be followed in actual therapies. The next chapter discusses in more detail adaptations made in the treatment of specific mental disorders with mindfulness-based interventions.

Chapter 4

Mindfulness and mental disorder

Tout le malheur des hommes vient d'une seule chose, qui est de ne savoir pas demeurer en repos dans une chambre.
(Usual translation: 'All man's miseries derive from being unable to sit quietly in a room alone.')

Blaise Pascal, *Pensées*, 2/139

Mindfulness and psychological distress

In what ways do these different therapeutic uses of mindfulness affect mental health? It is clear from Chapter 3 that different approaches have different kinds of aims. None are necessarily identical with the intentions that motivated the traditional practices discussed in Chapter 1. In many cases, goals that were quite specific, problem-orientated, and measurable have been chosen as the rationale of the mindfulness-based treatment. Conventional wisdom has it that psychological treatments, like physical ones, are used to treat mental disorders, such as major depression, obsessional compulsive neurosis, or schizophrenia. People diagnosed as suffering from depression must need an antidepressant or a specific psychological treatment for the condition.

However well this may work in the prescription of physical treatments, when it comes to psychotherapies, this strategy is suspect on several counts (cf. Guthrie 2000). The simplest is that there are likely to be much more reliable factors that distinguish the people who are likely to benefit from a particular intervention from those who do not than their diagnosis. The experience of mindfulness-based cognitive therapy (MBCT) could be taken as a case in point here. The very rigorous conditions under which it was evaluated mean it is possible to discriminate with considerable precision when it appears to be clinically useful and when it is not. Indeed, if the results from the original trial are simply used to answer the question, 'Is MBCT helpful to people with a diagnosis of depression?', the answer would appear to be 'no', because the numbers who did not benefit dilute the impact of those who did. More people would have had to be included in the study for the latter's positive influence to be convincing. It is also apparent how misleading it would be to say the study shows the intervention is not effective. The question really needs to be, 'When is MBCT helpful?', in which case the consistent answer has been, in that study and in a replication study (Ma and Teasdale 2004), 'when people have had three or more episodes of depression'.

In practice, specific data allowing this kind of question to be answered are rarely available. What is always available is some account of what the users of a treatment were seeking relief from, and a professional's view of how it was expected to help. These objectives are often more specific than the terminology of diagnosis, being likely to be influenced by a mixture of theoretical considerations about how a treatment is supposed to work, as well as clinical experience (personal or reported) of what it actually achieves.

It is possible to categorise the likely impacts of mindful therapies in a way that takes this into account. The following schema, which is illustrative rather than exhaustive, has basic units that are also closer to subjective experience and to what people are likely to say they want help for:

Mood	anxiety; depression; anger
Intrusions	ruminations; hallucinations; memories
Behaviours	binging; substance dependence; physical self-harm; violence
Problems of relating	negative attitudes to others; lack of empathy
Problems of self	self-consciousness; poor self-esteem; self-hatred

In the remainder of this chapter, we shall be looking selectively at the contribution of mindfulness to alleviation of mental disorders. Individual examples are likely to involve at least one, and often more than one, experienced difficulty from this list. While the history of using mindfulness with a range of somatic conditions, from fibromyalgia to psoriasis, will not be discussed here, it would be exceedingly dualistic to insist on a sharp division between the two kinds of illness. In the previous chapter, the holistic origins and aims of MBSR were mentioned. When it was used in a study of anxiety disorders published in a psychiatric journal, the subjects being reported on were medical patients attending a general hospital (Kabat-Zinn et al. 1992). It was one of many papers that have noted the high psychological morbidity among such patients, although those that go on to describe acceptable and effective treatments are relatively rare. The impact of MBSR in medical settings poses interesting questions about how far it is possible to detach effects on physical and mental well-being. In the qualitative study described in Chapter 2, focus group participants described personal experiences in the face of pain and illness. They agreed that its helpfulness in overcoming anxiety and fear had been critical in those situations. The attempt to concentrate exclusively on mental ill health in this chapter may therefore seem artificial.

Anxiety disorders

Pathological anxiety is recognised by the appearance of physical as well as psychological symptoms. The physical symptoms include sweating, shortness of breath, palpitations and nausea; the psychological ones are typified by worry, fear for the future and dread. These occur in many permutations, with a particular combination of physical and psychological anxiety being typical for each individual, and likely to be repeated as anxiety recurs. When anxiety takes the form of acute panic attacks, the bodily signs can become the basis for conscious fears, such as a belief that the sufferer is about to collapse or even die. Diagnosticians look for the specific features of phobias (anxiety associated with a particular object or situation, linked to their avoidance), panic attacks (acute and disabling attacks of anxiety with a considerable physical component), and the obsessions and compulsions that are characteristic of obsessional compulsive disorder. If none of these are prominent, the anxiety may be attributed to generalised anxiety disorder (GAD). It is likely to be harder to attribute the anxiety to particular precipitants with GAD, while the prognosis from all forms of treatment is also relatively poorer. In many situations, anxiety is inevitable: it is as abnormal to fail to feel it as to feel it to an extent that is truly handicapping. Health will lie in a capacity to tolerate normal levels of anxiety rather than its banishment.

Once mindfulness-based stress reduction (MBSR) had been developed, anxiety was the first specifically mental health issue to be examined. Kabat-Zinn *et al.* (1992) measured the symptomatic impact of MBSR on symptoms of anxiety (including panic attacks) in people who had volunteered to undergo the usual training package at general hospitals. (There was no control group.) They all therefore had concomitant medical conditions, many of them being likely to be sources of anxiety in themselves. Significant improvements in measures of anxiety (and depression) were recorded by the end of the programme. They were sustained at a follow-up 3 years later (Miller *et al.* 1995), when the majority of people involved in the follow-up had continued to practise mindfulness since its conclusion. (Numbers were too small to permit analyses of the possible effect of the regularity or amount of practice.) The authors have emphasised the differences between this approach and traditional cognitive therapy. As well as pointing to the non-cognitive nature of the somatic focusing on which it relies, they remind us that the intervention was never intended to change or 'restructure' particular thoughts. The process of engagement had been quite different, following which MBSR was seen as setting a broader kind of enquiry in process. Its consequences included, but were not restricted to, anxiety reduction. Technically, the study had not included an independent marker of 'mindfulness', and it is therefore possible that any of the contextual factors that the authors have highlighted could have contributed to the observed clinical improvements.

Observations made by this group on another group of medical patients also have considerable implications for the future use of mindfulness-based interventions in people with anxiety. After selecting 74 people from a cohort whose anxiety levels were above average, Kabat-Zinn *et al.* (1997) found that a subgroup of nine had predominantly cognitive symptoms of anxiety. In 20 others, anxiety had a heavily somatic expression, being mixed in the remainder. The investigators enquired systematically into the preferences of the 29 people whose expression was clearly cognitive or somatic, for different techniques within the MBSR programme. Yoga was seen by the investigators as the most somatically focused exercise, and sitting meditation as the most cognitive, with the body scan as intermediate between the two. Whereas Kabat-Zinn and colleagues had hypothesised that people with cognitive symptoms seek and prefer cognitive techniques for anxiety reduction, they found the opposite. The nine participants with a cognitive pattern of anxiety tended to prefer yoga to sitting meditation; the 20 with marked somatic anxiety symptoms, the reverse. The benefits of the programme were broadly comparable for all groups. This finding supports the introduction of a variety of techniques within the mindfulness training programme and the encouragement that is given to participants to make a personal selection from these. The complementarity this study indicates between presenting symptoms and mindfulness methods has not been formally tested in a comparative study of outcomes.

No formal studies of mindfulness-based interventions appear to have been conducted specifically on people with phobias, although mindfulness was one component of the work of Schwartz *et al.* (1996) on obsessional compulsive disorder. Although effective, evidence-based treatments exist for both of these conditions already, it would be reasonable to expect mindfulness to potentiate the impact of exposure-based treatments if it helps people to overcome experiential avoidance.

Generalised anxiety, however, and the incessant conscious worry that goes with it, has been more refractory to other treatment approaches. Roemer, Orsillo and colleagues at Boston have given considerable thought to the functions of worry in devising a multicomponent, 16-week treatment programme that combines features of MBCT, DBT and ACT in the treatment of generalised anxiety. Preliminary results from a randomised controlled trial (Roemer *et al.* 2006) suggest that it is at least as effective as existing cognitive treatments, but it will only be possible to consider the role of individual components once the study is complete.

Depression

The mood changes of depression have received considerable attention. Depression is recognised as a clinical problem once a tendency to sadness, tearfulness and apathy starts to take on a life of its own, and becomes a serious obstacle to getting on with ordinary activities. As well as reduced interest in things that ordinarily bring pleasure, including eating and sex, sleep is disrupted and is less refreshing. A daily pattern of mood change may become evident, with greatest intensity of depression at a particular time each day (especially early in the morning). Thoughts are consistently pessimistic, with ideas about oneself and the past becoming negative and coupled with a tendency to dwell on the past rather than the present or the future. Concentration is impaired, with greater difficulty in maintaining attention – an effect that seems closely related to sleep disruption. Progression of these features can lead to a state of profound slowing of movements and speech; loss of interest in others and in ordinary routines; and increasingly fixed ideas of failure, hopelessness and possibly guilt. These may be coupled with thoughts of death, self-harm and suicidal acts.

Links between depressed mood and attentiveness have long been recognised. The impairment of concentration that is frequently reported commonly refers to an inability to maintain concentration (and short-term memory) through ordinary tasks. Patients may take much longer than usual to read a newspaper article, and then complain they cannot recall anything they have just read. Apart from a general apathy, the withdrawal of interest from others during depression has been noted and was the basis of Freud's psychodynamic observations concerning the narcissistic basis of melancholia (Freud 1920). Freud describes how attention is withdrawn from others in the real world in favour of an internal object that is not only felt to be absent but, like a missing tooth in the mouth, becomes an overriding preoccupation. Another important observation concerns the apparent paradox of depressed people's visible lethargy and the restlessness of their thinking processes. The persistence of depressive thinking once symptomatic remission has been otherwise achieved has been an important aspect of the 'residual symptoms' of depression that have been shown to identify people at greater risk of future relapse (Fava 2000).

Although both cognitive therapy based on the work of A. T. Beck and interpersonal therapy (IPT) have been successful in trials in the treatment of individual episodes, they have not necessarily prevented the increase in the risk of becoming depressed that is seen with each successive episode. The relative risk of relapse in depression for a given number of past episodes is also known to be greater among people whose recovery is incomplete, leaving them with residual symptoms such as the social withdrawal and depressive attitudes that Fava described. This indicates that a psychological process could be directly linked to the continuing vulnerability to relapse.

Unipolar depression was taken by Teasdale, Williams and Segal as the paradigm of a common, chronic, relapsing mood disorder that might be helped by mindfulness-based treatment. As mentioned in Chapter 3, their MBCT was effectively designed as an intervention package for people who, while currently well (and enjoying unimpaired concentration), were at risk of further relapse. Two well-matched cohorts of people who had been depressed on at least two occasions as adults were randomised to treatment with MBCT or treatment as usual. Although the study was designed to determine whether there was a difference between the capacity of these treatments to prevent future relapse, it did not lead to a simple 'yes' or 'no'. Instead, initial stratification of the sample into a majority who had been depressed three times or more, and smaller groups in each condition who had been depressed only twice, led to separate reporting of the results for each subgroup. They have been dramatically different, with MBCT significantly reducing the risk of relapse compared to usual treatment in people having three or more depressive episodes, whereas there has been no difference for people having only two past episodes in either the original study or a smaller replication study (Ma and Teasdale 2004).

It has been noted that the risk of relapse for patients receiving 'treatment as usual' is greater according to the number of previous episodes they have had. MBCT has the effect of keeping the risk of relapse stable among patients experiencing more than three episodes, however many episodes they have had. Moreover, the level at which it stabilises is little more than where it ordinarily stands after two episodes with treatment as usual. This suggests that, whatever mechanism may be at play, MBCT effectively neutralises a potent factor that otherwise increases future risk of relapse.

The main trial sheds little light on this directly. (It was also so much in advance of its time that no measures of patients' attainments in mindfulness in response to the training could be included.) However, all three principal investigators were distinguished psychopathologists who had already thought extensively about depression and the ways in which metacognitive changes could have observable clinical consequences. A substudy conducted with the Welsh participants in the main trial also showed that MBCT reduced overgeneral autobiographical memory among such formerly depressed patients (Williams *et al.* 2000). In a parallel study on the participants from Canada and Cambridge, Teasdale *et al.* (2002) devised a marker of 'metacognitive awareness' that could be given to participants in both study groups after the MBCT subjects had received their intervention during the second year of the follow-up period. With it, Teasdale attempted to gauge the extent to which subjects would demonstrate what he calls 'metacognitive insight' when they are exposed to depressive thoughts following a negative stimulus. One explanation of why some people respond at such a juncture by relapsing into full-blown depression and others do not is that the relapsers react to such depressive thoughts as if they were literally true and/or part of them. Non-relapsers, using an ability to access a different metacognitive set, are much less troubled because, without having to rationalise or resist, they simply do not identify with the negative thoughts. However, instead of accessing responses to actual events, Teasdale's test of metacognition elicited an auto-biographical memory with a probe before recording the subjects' account of their feelings. Independent raters then assessed the metacognitive awareness that was displayed.

The same instrument had been used to rate metacognitive aware-ness both before and after treatment of patients in another trial with residual depression by orthodox cognitive therapy (Paykel *et al.* 1999). They had shown a small but significant improvement in metacognitive capacity relative to patients who did not have the orthodox cognitive therapy. Despite methodological weaknesses, Teasdale concluded that the studies suggested not only that MBCT could exert its effects, as hypothesised, through changes in subjects' relationship to cognitions rather than their content, but also that this might be an important mode of action of other forms of cog-nitive therapy in depression.

In clinical terms, the rationale of using mindfulness to prevent relapse of depression concerns the role of rumination, or persistent and automatic elaboration of negative thoughts concerning oneself and how one should be. Rumination was identified as a factor in prolonging depressive episodes by Nolen-Hoeksema (Nolen-Hoeksema and Morrow 1991, 1993), being operationalised along with three other coping styles (distraction, problem-solving, and dangerous activities) in the Response Styles Questionnaire (RSQ) (Nolen-Hoeksema and Morrow 1991). The effect of mindfulness in reducing depressive ruminations appears to be robust, being repli-cated by Ramel *et al.* (2004). MBCT's role in relation to depressive ruminations is hypothesised to bring about a general switch in 'mental mode'. Accordingly, mindfulness brings about a 'decenter-ing' in relation to each successive experience that is incompatible with the chain reactions characteristic of the ordinary mental mode. If depressive ruminations no longer receive the kind of reactive attention that allows them to amplify, the negative mood changes that are usually consequent on this will be prevented (cf. Segal *et al.* 2002: 75).

Anger and emotional regulation

Unwelcome emotion is far from exhausted by anxiety and depression, although these two are highlighted by conventional classifications of mental disorder. In psychotherapeutic practice, however, difficulty in controlling anger, internally or toward others, is a common complaint. It is interesting how prominent the topic can be in the self-help books renowned Buddhist teachers, such as Thich Nhat Hanh or the Dalai Lama, write for Western audiences (e.g. Lama 1997; Hanh 2002) while it receives little direct attention in the Western mindfulness literature. Yet empirical studies confirm that unresolved anger commonly underlies anxiety symptoms and depression (Bloch *et al.* 1993). Much practical therapeutic experience is summed up in Neborsky's (2006) comment: 'Studies of improvement [in intensive short-term psychotherapy] show ability to access sad feelings reduces symptoms and ability to access anger correlates with character change' (Neborsky 2006: 526).

Excessive and uncontrolled anger is a recognised feature of borderline personality disorder (BPD). A simple rationalisation of this would be to see it as one aspect of a general impulsivity, in which urges to gratify sexual, oral, or attachment needs are relatively unrestrained, with violence, promiscuity, clinging, bingeing and substance misuse being more likely. However, the concept of emotional regulation has become popular as a way of accounting for emotional volatility and evident difficulty in containing aggression by attributing it to failures in neurodevelopment as well as early psychological care (Schore 1994). This has been influential in the treatment philosophy of dialectical behaviour therapy (DBT) (Linehan 1993a) and the importance that education has assumed within the model as part of the process of validating clients' experience. Mindfulness has been used as the key to a successful intervention in reducing aggression on the part of a learning-disabled adult (Singh *et al.* 2003). As the paper's colourful title suggests, this was through a deliberate deflection of attention when angry feelings arose to the soles of his feet.

Behaviours: binge eating

Mindfulness has been incorporated into two treatments that have been used with demonstrable success with people who binge. DBT has been used primarily with binge eating disorder rather than bulimia nervosa (Telch *et al.* 2001). The adaptation of DBT has involved reorganisation of group training sessions, with downplaying of the personal therapeutic component. Core skills in mindfulness, emotion regulation, and distress tolerance are taught in sequence. Although one guiding rationale for this was that bingeing behaviour is a means of affect regulation, the female subjects evaluated after treatment showed no real change in their affective state, although they made considerable improvements in bingeing behaviour, largely maintained at 6-month follow-up. It has appeared that patients' ability not to react to negative affect was strengthened, indicating the importance of the cultivation of mindfulness within the programme. However, no independent measures of mindfulness have been used in the course of evaluation.

Mindfulness-based eating awareness training (MB–EAT) (Kristeller and Hallett 1999) has also been used with binge eating disorder. Each has adopted a different rationale, and modified its process for use with this client group. Kristeller and Hallet adapted MBCT to highlight cognitions concerning eating behaviour. Clients believed exercises focusing on these were particularly helpful. Analyses of therapeutic effects have suggested that enhancing sensitivity to internal satiety cues is particularly important, a finding that has subsequently influenced the model. The introduction of meditation to foster feelings of forgiveness (to counter the feelings of guilt commonly encountered with this population) has also been favourably received. Baer and colleagues (Kristeller *et al.* 2006) have recently reported that, when successful, MB–EAT increases clients' mindfulness and decreases their belief that they would lose control if they refrained from bingeing.

Substance misuse

A different mindfulness-based approach has been used with considerable success in the management of substance misuse. Like the 12-step programmes within Alcoholics Anonymous and Narcotics Anonymous, it demands a different sort of commitment than most therapies, aiming to get to the roots of someone's motivation and dependence. Marlatt *et al.* (2004) have actively arranged programmes whereby people with severe dependence can enter a residential programme based upon a very traditional Buddhist meditation retreat. This involves living alongside others in silence, except for interactions with the teacher, and meditating from 4 am until midevening through a 10-day period. The meditation, based upon the Burmese vipassana school of S. N. Goenka, involves exclusive attention to the breath over the first 3 days before introduction of mindfulness to body sensations. This is interspersed with daily 'dhamma talks', in which recorded seminars covering the basics of Buddhist philosophy and the rationale of the meditations are screened. As might be inferred from Chapter 1, these provide an analysis in which craving is a virtually universal habit that cannot be overcome directly because of the nature of mental proliferation. However, it can be reversed through a gradual psychological purification that the meditations facilitate. Although the spartan and intense regime is unusually challenging, Marlatt has been pleasantly reassured by the determination that most entrants to the programme have shown. He has also organised treatment programmes of this kind within custodial institutions: the immediate results in terms of inmates' behaviour change have meant that the considerable disruption of running such a programme within a secure institution has been willingly tolerated by the authorities.

The other approach, of 'mindfulness-based relapse prevention', has involved direct adaptation from MBSR (Witkiewitz *et al.* 2005), some of the experiences in developing MB–EAT being taken into account. The use of mindfulness to enhance internal sensitivity as well as a more disengaged interest in urges to use substances follows naturally from these authors' long-standing interest in relapse prevention, and the use of mindfulness to facilitate early recognition of individual relapse signatures. The use of mindfulness-based group treatments with attenders of a residential programme has been of additional interest, as the immediate impact of the programme on mediators of the stress response has been demonstrated through significant reductions in salivary cortisol (Marcus *et al.* 2003).

Suicidal behaviour

The impulsive and autoaggressive actions that lead to drug overdose and deliberate self-injury can be considered separately from the mood changes of depression. These behaviours are common among people diagnosed with BPD, but have also proven to be the most tractable aspect of that syndrome when DBT is offered. The finding of consistent and lasting reduction in suicidal behaviour accounted for much of the interest with which the first evaluation was received (Linehan *et al.* 1991) and has remained when evaluation has been more rigorous and statistically robust (Linehan *et al.* 2006).

The clinical importance of suicide prevention has also served to refine ideas on the probable contribution of mindfulness here in terms of its action and timing. Williams and Swales (2004) refer to DBT as a 'stage one' treatment, offering practical support and techniques for regaining personal control when suicidal urges are acute. Other techniques are combined with mindfulness in order to bring this about. However, they feel that more purely mindfulness-based measures are likely to be helpful subsequently. People who are prone to suicidal acts are prone to distorted evaluations of their situation, especially where perceptions of entrapment are concerned. (It appears that cognitive habits rather than events have more and more of a role to play as suicidal behaviour becomes more chronic.) These authors hypothesise that the capacity of people to resist suicidal impulses rationally is also challenged because their problem-solving capacity is impaired through a combination of overgeneral memory and depressive rumination. The kind of mindfulness practice that MBCT supports, in robbing depressive rumination of its potency through differential activation of a decentred mode of experiencing, would therefore have significant potential in preventing future suicidal actions. This important hypothesis is being evaluated in clinical studies.

Intrusions: hallucinations and delusions

People diagnosed with psychotic illnesses frequently suffer from mental intrusions in the form of hallucinations (fully formed sensory experiences that do not correspond with other people's perceptions of external events) and delusions (recurrent thoughts that are bizarre or irrational but which the person is inclined to believe). These can be the source of a good deal of distress, as can the poor circumstances in which many people having illnesses like schizophrenia live. Previous treatment strategies of cognitive-behavioural therapy have tended to concentrate either on reduction of these symptoms or on the enhancement of coping skills that would reduce distress and improve functioning by dealing with concomitant problems with adjustment, self-image, social functioning and motivation. Two different mindfulness-based strategies have now been used with some success with this patient group, the differences between them mirroring the contrast between those earlier approaches.

In the UK, Chadwick *et al.* (2005) have used a kind of mindfulness training, modified to their patients' circumstances, based on breathing meditation. After an initial session in which attention is focused by a brief body scan, mindfulness of breathing is used in sessions and between them to develop patients' ability to reduce anxiety prior to attempts to face negative, intrusive experiences directly and with acceptance. Because there can be inaccurate beliefs about the experiences (for instance, that they are caused by another, persecutory, person), acceptance here will involve recognising their transience, and letting them pass without getting caught in ruminations or judgements about them. The intervention has been offered during short sessions (no longer than 90 minutes including a break) with no more than 10 minutes' meditation practice at a time. These are interspersed with regular comments and instructions so that no extended silent periods are imposed. Home practice is optional, and audio tapes are supplied so that it, too, would not be entirely silent if attempted. The sessions also include didactic material about aspects of mindfulness, such as letting go, and how to use them in specific situations, and attempts to use mindfulness with difficult experiences are discussed at the start of the next session. The first 11 people to complete such classes have been evaluated for symptom changes (significantly improved) and their impact on their ability to use mindfulness (using the Mindfulness Questionnaire; cf. Chapter 2). This indicated a greater learned ability to use mindfulness with distressing thoughts and images than with voices. The approach was clearly new to all concerned, but did not appear to increase their distress, while replies to a third evaluation measure indicated that they saw mindfulness as the most active ingredient in the whole group experience.

All components of ACT were brought into play in work that used it with inpatients having chronic psychosis (Bach and Hayes 2002; Bach *et al.* 2006). Commitment to work toward agreed goals based on patients' values was introduced from the outset, while no view was expressed on the desirability of symptomatic change. Without any formal meditative practices, patients would be encouraged to experience intrusive thoughts and sensations as they actually were, rather than in terms of ideas that patients had about them. To do this, classic ACT exercises, such as using the image of 'soldiers (moving) in a line' to practise disidentification from thoughts (which can then be carried away on the soldiers' rifles), are introduced. Especially if there is evidence of concomitant cognitive impairment, these may be explained and rehearsed in a more literal fashion than with other patients, such as a demonstration with toy soldiers. There is also an interest in looking at delusions in terms of their possible function in relation to other aspects of the patients; that is, how they may serve as a means of experiential avoidance in themselves. One of the characteristic features of ACT is the interest in 'self as context'. In the case of people with psychosis, this may involve the encouragement of verbal self-description in order to enhance self-awareness, which is also more likely to be impaired than among other groups. Evaluations of this intervention included a randomised trial that demonstrated longer intervals before readmission compared to treatment as usual, although there was no symptomatic improvement (Bach and Hayes 2002). The study was repeated to ensure professional attention was equivalent between groups, with a positive trend toward reduction of risk of rehospitalisation and clear evidence of symptomatic change (Bach et al. 2006). It is obviously harder to assess the contribution of 'mindfulness' in a complex intervention of this kind, and no independent assessments of patients' mindfulness have been made.

Trauma

Trauma is commonly associated with intrusive experiences in the form of extremely vivid memories, which appear suddenly while waking or asleep, and which fail to change from appearance to appearance. Other common, subsequent effects of trauma include phobic anxiety, amnesia, emotional and bodily numbing, and high states of arousal associated with a vigilant attention in which the horizon is being continually scanned for signs of further danger. One definition of a traumatic experience is one that 'defines the way people organize their subsequent perceptions' (Van der Kolk 2002: 60). Van der Kolk is referring to the domination of experience by traumatic memory to the extent that it is clear both to sufferers and to an observer that their perception is dominated by their past because of its content, focus and the habitually fearful reactions that meet it. (This is a most interesting definition in the light of the traditional Buddhist psychology discussed in Chapter 1. According to that, all perceptions are likely to structure future ones through conditioning!) 'Trauma' is therefore a question of degree, with some perceptual reoganisations being more evident than others.

Practically speaking, trauma is a hugely important subject. It has been said that the final measure of any doctor is how well they help others cope with pain. Trauma is a similar test for any psychotherapist. It is one that, while instrumental in bringing many psychotherapeutic innovations to broader attention, from psychoanalysis through behaviour therapy to eye movement desensitisation and reprocessing (EMDR), no one has necessarily mastered. And there is not yet a widely accepted mindfulness-based treatment for trauma. A recent book on mindfulness and psychotherapy (Germer *et al.* 2005) has only three pages on the subject, not all of those strictly about trauma. Yet, not only is trauma common, but it is also a major issue in the use of mindfulness-based training. Past traumatic experiences that have been coped with by suppression are likely to be reactivated through exercises in which subjects are invited deliberately to turn their attention inward. This is especially likely because of a tendency for memories of traumatic events to have been associated with physical sensations. When deliberate, focused attention is moved around the body, relative anaesthesia can give way to re-experiencing of these sensations, with a return of the strong affects and images accompanying the original traumatising experience. This has implications even for non-clinical settings. Many teachers offering classes in mindfulness techniques take care to check whether prospective participants have a history of trauma. When offering a sample taste of mindfulness to a group of conference attenders or colleagues, some teachers prefer to use a form of sitting meditation rather than an exercise such as Kabat-Zinn's 'body scan', in which focused awareness of all areas of the body is invited. Within clinical practice, the emergence of traumatic memories, whether expected or not, remains an area of considerable practical concern.

Where practitioners have helped others to reprocess traumatic experience in the course of MBSR, they have made significant technical adaptations, such as helping their students at the outset to establish a safe place to which they can withdraw at any time at will. This may then be augmented by other devices that help people modulate their attention, rather than focusing it inward and exclusively on the traumatic material. These can include keeping the eyes open and keeping up a verbal commentary on the unfolding experience, as in 'Now I'm doing x . . .'.

Mindfulness is of course also a core component of approaches such as DBT and ACT. Many people receiving DBT will be known to be traumatised. As in the discussion of acute suicidal behaviour, both approaches, in mixing mindfulness with other, more overtly ego-supportive techniques, have a capacity to enhance current coping and prepare people for subsequent internal exploration before it is introduced. The same probably applies to the use of positive affect in Gilbert's compassionate mind training (Gilbert 2005), another example that mindfulness practitioners are likely to follow in practice. It is not surprising that when new packages incorporating mindfulness have been designed to assist people presenting with trauma, they have included a full range of supportive as well as exploratory techniques. This is also true of Wolfs-dorf and Zlotnick's work with adult survivors of childhood sexual abuse, in which mindfulness is encouraged within identification and management of affects, particularly anger, while exposure to traumatic memories is resisted within this 'stage one' treatment (Wolfsdorf and Zlotnick 2001).

There are reports in the literature of the successful use of mindfulness training with traumatised patients (Urbanowski and Miller 1996). In them, so-called concentrative meditative techniques are regularly used to stabilise awareness, and to provide a way of returning to awareness of present experience through, for instance, awareness of the breath, before more free-ranging mindful awareness is encouraged. Indeed, several of the patients reported had considerable prior experiences of such meditative techniques that, it was acknowledged, helped to prepare them for experiencing traumatic memories during mindful therapy. The object of this was essentially to bring an accepting attitude in place of the aversion that had served to maintain the intensity and isolation of the memories. (The risk of introducing an open, mindful mindset was that, instead of feared memories taking their place alongside all the other components of experience, they would flood clients' awareness to the exclusion of anything else, reinforcing their isolation and affective charge.) Practical precautions also included building up tolerance of distress, in the context of the helping relationship, before an attempt was made to focus inwards on painful areas by mindfulness techniques. However, what is striking in this account is the additional reliance on 'light trance' to introduce a sense of distance from the experiences that are then revived and worked through in the course of an intense dialogue between therapist and client. Whether the reported use of trance has made an active contribution here or not, it will not remove the sense of risk that attaches to mindfulness within the psychotherapy of trauma.

Finally, a distinctive, if relatively untested, therapeutic approach to trauma is offered by Ogden and Minton (2000). In what they term 'sensorimotor psychotherapy', they apply mindfulness with distinctive methods and objectives in order to reverse the dissociation they attribute the effects of trauma to:

> Mindfulness is the key to clients becoming more and more acutely aware of internal sensorimotor reactions and in increasing their capacity for self-regulation. Mindfulness is a state of consciousness in which one's awareness is directed toward here-and-now internal experience, with the intention of simply observing rather than changing this experience. Therefore, we can say that mindfulness engages the cognitive faculties of the client in support of sensorimotor processing, rather than allowing bottom-up trauma-related processes to escalate and take control of information processing. To teach mindfulness, the therapist asks questions that require mindfulness to answer, such as, 'What do you feel in your body? Where exactly do you experience tension? What sensation do you feel in your legs right now? What happens in the rest of your body when your hand makes a fist?' Questions such as these force the client to come out of a dissociated state and future- or past-centered ideation and experience the present moment through the body. Such questions also encourage the client to step back from being embedded in the traumatic experience and to report [instead] from the standpoint of an observing ego, an ego that 'has' an experience in the body rather than 'is' that bodily experience.
>
> (Ogden and Minton 2000)

In working with a traumatised patient, they constantly monitor the patient's arousal. Whenever this seems likely to go beyond what is tolerable, further questions are asked to help the patient redirect attention to sensations, to the exclusion of feeling or thoughts. They acknowledge that a capacity to do this is crucial; otherwise, the patient's personal tolerance is likely to be exceeded. This tolerance can be quite limited, and the impact of exceeding it particularly destabilising among people who are seen as internally disorganised. It could mean jeopardising their existing ability to maintain awareness away from the traumatic content. The aims that Ogden and Minton describe, in developing an exclusive awareness of sensorimotor experience, seem very compatible with traditional accounts of 'mindfulness of the body'. Their own procedure involves patients not only becoming fully aware of sensation at that level, but also developing a vocabulary in their discussions with the therapist for this somatic experience, independent of feelings and interpretations. (These can be added later if necessary.)

Given the wealth of experience that is available from the meditative traditions in cultivating the power to observe selectively but minutely, and in naming experiences (as part of letting them pass), it is curious that these authors do not seem to have recommended any exercises to build up these capacities in advance of the therapeutic sessions. Their emphasis on maintaining a somatic focus, and on ensuring it is exclusive as a way of modulating affect where necessary, appears to be unique in the therapeutic literature. (As they point out, the somatic focusing advocated by Gendlin (cf. Chapter 3) invites simultaneous opening to somatic, emotional and cognitive components. Their method is deliberately designed to avoid this.)

The approach represented by sensorimotor psychotherapy seems promising. Its emphasis on naming and describing aside, it has much in common with the kind of traditional vipassana techniques, emphasising mindfulness of the body, that Marlatt's substance misusers were able to tolerate. Moreover, paying close and exclusive attention to bodily sensations as a way of innoculating against anticipated trauma was a personal strategy used by several of the participants in the exploratory focus group reported in Chapter 2. They were in no doubt that its success was greatly assisted by regular prior meditative practice. If sensorimotor psychotherapy proves to have consistent positive effects, these seem likely to be potentiated by regular practice of the key mindfulness skills it requires. It also deserves more formal evaluation of its clinical effects.

Relationships

Destructive relationships have been a traditional focus of psychotherapeutic work, often in the context of other difficulties such as
mood disorders. Mindfulness has been applied in both individual
and couple treatments to address underlying difficulties. James
Carson and colleagues have developed mindfulness-based relationship enhancement (MBRE) as a couples intervention that is based
upon and retains the essential structure of MBSR (Carson et al.
2004). It differs from MBSR in the way, from intake onward,
couples work together in going through the programme. The content is adjusted to facilitate this, with yoga sessions making use of
conjoint exercises, and additional exercises being introduced to
augment bodily sensitivity through mindful touch. A departure
from the usual balance of exercises is an emphasis on the practice
on loving kindness in meditation throughout the course. At other
times, attention to directing and receiving positive feelings with the
partner is incorporated, as in a silent two-phase, eye-gazing exercise. Recognition and acceptance of feelings that are sensed in
phase one are followed by focus on 'deep-down goodness' within
both parties in phase two. In Carson's evaluation of this package,
measures of acceptance, distress and happiness within the
relationship have shown changes in the expected directions. Their
rating of 'closeness' did not appear to respond (Carson et al. 2006).

The self

This domain of traditional psychotherapy is not one that has, as
yet, been opened up through clinical demonstrations of a specific
effect for mindfulness in areas of self pathology. Indeed, although
people with BPD or psychotic mental states have major difficulties
with internal integration and their subjective sense of agency, there
appears to be little evidence as yet that these aspects benefit directly
from mindfulness-based approaches. Indeed, weakness of self-
structure can be seen as a contraindication for their use, as it is to
many meditative practices. Versions of the classic advice to the
would-be meditator, that the ego needs to attain a certain strength
before it can be softened, can also be heard in clinical settings.

On the other hand, there are few psychotherapies that, unless
they are extremely superficial, do not engage a complicated network

of self-judgements and sensitivities that are inseparable from someone's feeling of individuality. When these go on being elaborated as someone becomes very moody, withdrawn, fearful, or hyperactive in a way that makes others feel they must be ill, it makes the impact of what is happening worse. And it can make the person affected more likely to resist offers of help rather than welcoming them. In an apparently unassuming paper on 'depression, low self-esteem and mindfulness', that recognises low self-esteem as the manifestation of an enduring difficulty in people's relationship to themselves that exacerbates depression, Fennell (2004) maps out a continuum of treatment difficulty. It is a map that would apply across different treatment approaches. According to it, people who are relatively easy to treat have relatively specific, acute problems in the context of a previously well-functioning self where any negative internal perspectives are counterbalanced by positive ones. People who are relatively difficult to treat have multiple, diffuse, long-standing difficulties that they identify with, in the context of a dysfunctional self (with chronic feelings of low self-esteem) from which positive self-perspectives are effectively absent. When it comes to the use of mindfulness to assist recovery, Fennell uses the concept of decentering to identify the crucial step in each case. In easier-to-treat patients, decentering from depression (as taught in MBCT) should be sufficient. In the chronic, harder-to-treat patients, she sees the core task in terms of trying to create an entirely new view of the self, rather than strengthening a pre-existing one. Mindfulness has to be brought to bear on people's entire view of themselves, as part of a radical exercise in decentering from low self-esteem. The difficulties of this are not underestimated. The sense of personal threat it engenders is likely to be expressed in many ways, including resistance to working with the therapist, scepticism concerning the possibility or value of change, and failure to work as expected within the therapy.

These observations seem extremely important. They refer to the post-phase one treatment of many people who present to psychological therapy services after the failure of relatively simple treatments. As there are already many effective treatments for uncomplicated anxiety disorders and depression, it is this arena that the usefulness of mindfulness within psychotherapy is likely to receive its most critical tests – and an important opportunity to demonstrate either effects other approaches do not offer, or those that would otherwise require much more elaborate or costly arrangements.

Adverse effects of mindfulness practice

It must not be assumed that all of the clinical consequences of mindfulness practice are necessarily positive or therapeutic. Attrition during trials of mindfulness-based interventions is rarely explored, and the whole question of side effects is under-researched. Known possible unintended effects that are exacerbated during intensive training retreats include restlessness, anxiety, depression, guilt and hallucinosis (Albeniz and Holmes 2000). The experienced practitioners described in Chapter 2 had also been asked about any adverse effects they had experienced. They reported restlessness, self-criticism and self-doubt during the early phases. One had also gone through a phase of being very judgemental toward others, while two had experienced forms of hallucinosis (auditory and visual) in retreat settings. It seems to be widely accepted that retreat settings are much more likely to precipitate perceptual disturbance, and experienced teachers may restrict access to them among meditators they believe to be vulnerable (VanderKooi 1997).

A number of significant reports of the negative effects of mindfulness exist in the older literature, including accounts of the precipitation of frank psychiatric illness. These include a well-documented case of mania (Yorston 2001) in apparent response to a brief experience of yoga and a zazen retreat, as well as reports of 'schizophrenia' that provide insufficient information about the phenomenology or the precipitants (Sethi and Bhargaa 2003). The one prospective study of side effects in long-term meditators is of most relevance, as, although it documents neither sensory disturbances nor frank illness, it was conducted with 27 'insight' meditators, that is, people practising mindfulness assessed after a meditation retreat (Shapiro 1992a). These subjects' previous experience at the time of the study ranged from nil to more than 7 years' experience of regular mindfulness meditation, although all had experience of formal meditation in some form. The effects reported were classified into three principal sorts:

1 *Intrapsychic.* These were by far the most common, being reported by half of Shapiro's sample. They comprised four kinds: 'negativity' (being judgemental, negative emotions, mental pain, and anxiety); 'disorientation' (confusion about self, low self-esteem, apathetic, and feeling incomplete); 'addicted to meditation'; and 'boredom and pain'.

2   *Interpersonal.* These ranged across family objections to
    meditators withdrawing for meditation, through being too
    aware of others' negative qualities (and judging these or feeling
    superior) to distress at recognising how bad their current
    family situation was.

3   *Societal adverse effects.* These included feelings of alienation as
    well as discomfort in everyday situations and difficulty in
    making practical adjustments.

Around 10 per cent of the sample reported effects under each of
items 1 and 2. In collecting these data, Deane Shapiro had asked
participants to identify for themselves whether an effect was
'adverse'. One of the most interesting findings was that adverse
effects were more rather than less common among the more
experienced meditators. Shapiro concluded that these must be
being offset by accumulating positive effects. This seemed to be
borne out by the reports of positive experiences that were requested
at the same time.

Shapiro reported elsewhere (1992b) that there was a strong
correlation between the likelihood of reporting of adverse effects
and participants' thoughts before the retreat began. There was also
a clear association between the length of participants' meditational
experience and their predominant motivation for meditating.
Assuming these cross-sectional findings can be used to infer a
progression over time, Shapiro concluded that motivation follows a
sequence in which an early wish for self-regulation is displaced by
one for self-exploration, and finally by one for self-liberation. This
suggests that motivation of the third kind may be associated with a
greater tolerance of discomfort and other apparently adverse
effects.

The therapeutic actions of mindfulness

A number of suggestions about how mindfulness helps in psychological treatments have been reported in these last two chapters.
Some ideas were criticised as being relatively indirect and of less
explanatory value than first appeared. They could also be developed in relation to a particular clinical problem (e.g. prophylaxis
of depression; improving self-regulation of affect) and remain
implicitly tied to that context, ignoring the potentially different
ways that mindfulness works in other situations. The present

chapter has reviewed some recent thinking about how mindfulness could have a positive impact on a number of quite different kinds of psychopathology, as well as the circumstances in which mindfulness itself seems most liable to be a source of difficulty. This should make it easier to think about clinical effects more inclusively, without these being overshadowed by a narrow range of psychopathology. Indeed, it seems possible to identify three ways in which mindfulness may have direct and potentially valuable effects across most clinical situations when it is practised by people with mental health problems.

The first way, building on some of Martin's (1997) observations, might be called 'dechaining'. It reflects the close, objective observation of psychological events that 'bare attention' brings. Not only is each event experienced in full detail, in a slowed-down way (as the concept of deautomatisation tried to indicate) but each event is also seen to be less firmly linked to those that precede and follow it than ordinary perception suggests. This loosening is more than a spacing out of perceptions, being a freeing up in which more alternatives become available. Examples of where this aspect is particularly important include the treatment of habit disorders.

The second way, building on the emphasis on exposure to be found in accounts of 'experiential avoidance' in ACT, represents a sort of exposure and might be called 'resensing'. The vitality of experience here reflects the absence of old reactions and reflects the capacity to welcome experiences with acceptance and equanimity as they are attended to, and a lack of fear and aversion. Examples of where this aspect is prominent in clinical situations include mindful therapy for anxiety and phobic disorders.

The third way, in recognition of the importance of mindfulness in bringing about perspectival shifts as people's relationship to their experience changes, is still probably best called 'decentering'. It is evident in a capacity to experience everything within awareness on the same basis, with a lessening of partial identifications (including those reinforced by linguistic habits). This aspect appears to be prominent when mindfulness-based approaches are used for problematic thoughts such as obsessional or depressive ruminations.

It seems unlikely that, if this analysis is adequate, the three ways will act in isolation of one another, or develop independently of the others in the course of mindfulness training. For instance, example 2 in the previous chapter (pp. 69–70) seems to bring about what

ACT refers to as 'cognitive defusion' through a combination of dechaining and decentering. If dechaining, resensing and decentering are basic actions of mindfulness in therapeutic contexts, it would seem sensible to use process measures that are sensitive to all three facets when evaluating treatments. It is also possible that therapeutic exercises used in mindfulness training may differentially develop one of these aspects more than the others.

It should be emphasised that these terms are trying to capture three intrinsic and therapeutically important actions of mindfulness, rather than secondary 'mindfulness skills'. The concept of mindfulness skills refers to the way mindful attention is deliberately gathered, applied or directed. It is also likely that the repertoire of clinically relevant mindfulness skills is different from what current accounts of them suggest. This is because greater precision about what is happening suggests that not everything that has been termed 'mindfulness' in clinical contexts deserves to have been. For instance, there are at least two other kinds of use of attention that are distinct from mindfulness, although closely related to it.

One is the kind of 'awareness of being aware' that comes into play when attention is directed across complex objects like body posture or when providing a verbal commentary to accompany actions. We saw in Chapter 1 how this would be designated as a knowing 'clear comprehension' that grows alongside mindful 'bare attention', but is not identical with it. It appears that the functional difference between these is actively exploited in packages like DBT, where 'mindfulness skills', such as describing, which have a clear and important role in fostering the capacity to attend, are more likely to enhance clear comprehension than bare attention.

The other instance is concentration, where attention is refocused in order to withdraw it from objects that are giving rise to dysphoric reactions, and to direct it instead on a restful object where an intensification of attention is likely to lead to inner feelings of peace and calm. Strictly speaking, this selective narrowing of attention to prevent exploration is not mindfulness, although the stratagem can be quite powerful, for instance, when working with traumatised patients. However, it is also possible to confuse it with mindfulness in practical situations where the outward instructions seem quite similar, even if the inner action is very different. Examples of this could be an inexperienced therapist's interpretation of the 3-minute breathing space in MBCT as the purposeful injection of a sense of calm (without paying attention to what was

going on), or a DBT therapist using 'mindfulness' simply to dis-
tract the patient's attention from anxiety-laden experiences onto an
innocuous object.

Although the claim that some attentional skills, such as describing, are mindfulness skills may be questionable, other abilities of
considerable therapeutic value may merit recognition as mindfulness skills instead. These might include directing awareness
outward in order to sense and register other people's feelings (cf.
the above discussion of mindfulness-based relationship enhancement) or narrowing the band of internally focused awareness in
order to explore, say, bodily sensations to the relative exclusion of
others (as in the earlier discussion of sensorimotor psychotherapy).

Conclusions

Mindfulness-based interventions have been used across a wide
range of psychological problems, including mood and anxiety
disorders, post-traumatic and psychotic symptoms, bingeing and
substance misuse, suicidal and impulsive actions, and difficulties in
relating. These differ considerably in the extent to which their
usefulness has been confirmed by formal outcome studies. The
severity of any of these clinical problems is likely to be influenced
by how far it is felt to be part of someone's self, different
therapeutic strategies being needed when this is the case. It is likely
that the capacity of mindful therapies to make a difference in more
severe and chronic cases will be important in determining their
long-term future. Mindfulness is also able to precipitate mental
disorders in rare cases, but it has a range of other potential side
effects that should also be considered in clinical contexts. The
clinical uses of mindfulness have often been rationalised through
explanatory models based on the pathogenic psychological processes that it affects. Consideration of these can be helpful in
refining ideas of the action of mindfulness. It is proposed that its
most direct therapeutic effects reflect three interdependent actions:
dechaining, resensing and decentering. A clear theory of action
seems essential for mindfulness to be recognised as a substantial
psychotherapeutic innovation.

Chapter 5

Harnessing mindfulness

Better than a thousand useless verses is one single verse that gives peace.

Dhammapada, verse 101 (Mascaro 1973: 50)

'In the seen will be merely what is seen; in the heard will be merely what is heard; in the sensed will be merely what is sensed; in the cognized will be merely what is cognized.' In this way you should train yourself, Bahiya.

Buddha's words to Bahiya Daruciriya, as related in the commentary to verse 101 of the *Dhammapada* (Khantipalo 1996: 123)

The last two chapters have mentioned a number of ways in which mindful awareness might be cultivated and maintained, concentrating on those that have been used in particular clinical contexts. As these have diversified, so has the range of techniques for becoming more mindful. Having a short attention span, being subjected to unusually insistent, intrusive phenomena, or having access to past experiences or body sensations restricted through internal defences can each make it particularly difficult to maintain a traditional practice for lengthy intervals of time. These limitations have been accommodated through some of the techniques discussed already in Chapters 3 and 4. As a result, there is a considerable menu of methods that have now been widely used in the development of mindfulness:

> **Techniques for experiencing mindfulness**
>
> *Formal practices*
> Sitting meditations
> *(mindfulness of breathing, body sensations, sounds, thoughts, etc.)*
> Movement meditations
> *(walking meditation, mindful yoga stretches)*
> Group exchange
> *(led exercises, guided discussion of experience)*
>
> *Informal practices*
> Mindful activity
> *(mindful eating, cleaning, driving, etc.)*
> Structured exercises
> *(thought dispersal, breathing space, etc.)*
> Contemplations
> *(poetry, aesthetic experiences)*

The traditional methods for developing mindfulness discussed in Chapter 1 have been augmented by others, both formal and informal. The current list is likely to be far from exhaustive. The preliminary study described in Chapter 2 has already indicated that research into how people actually acquire mindfulness could be particularly instructive in suggesting new methods, techniques and tips.

Changing gear – the role of mindfulness retreats

If there are so many potential ways of cultivating mindfulness, do any have a special place because they carry a promise of a greater intensity, depth or purity of experience? Is there any reliable way in which mindfulness might be maximised? One traditional answer is through the intensification of practice that a dedicated retreat provides. Whether such retreats last a day or a month, the following elements seem to be characteristic:

1   physical seclusion without regular contact with family, friends, or broadcast media

2   an environment that minimises distraction with simple decor, an unfussy (usually vegetarian) diet, segregated sleeping arrangements, etc.
3   long periods of continuing silence, usually with an early reveille to access full silence in the later hours of the night
4   rules restricting communication between participants – whether verbally, by signals, eye contact, etc.
5   rules restricting distracting activities such as reading, games, writing
6   a programme of formal practices based on alternating group sittings in mindful meditation and opportunities for mindful walking (other practices also possible)
7   some teaching and instruction, which may be provided completely separately from the practice sessions themselves
8   clear induction and leaving processes at the start and end of the retreat.

While it is easy to assume that the other aspects function to amplify the experience obtained during the formal practices listed at item 6 in this list, it is likely they are very potent modifiers of awareness in themselves. In representing a modulated form of sensory deprivation, they seem likely to encourage a greater awareness of events in the mind, before any specific meditative exercises are added. Once such exercises are under way, the structure is intended to prevent the immediate diffusion of changes in consciousness, engendering a (not necessarily welcome) continuity between exercise sessions, with a gradual intensification of any changes that result.

Apart from the synergy between milieu and the formal practices, attempts to identify just what lends retreats their intensity can also be confounded by the didactic, cognitive input (during induction, instruction sessions and *dhamma* talks) that places the practices in a framework of beliefs and expectations. As we saw in Chapter 1, motivation to undertake a practice is likely to be reinforced by beliefs that provide a rationale for it. These, in turn, will also influence details of procedure so that the practice is credible as a means of realising the desired goals. As we saw in the discussion of 'permeation' of mindfulness in Chapter 2, the new way of being aware gains momentum so that it becomes increasingly prevalent. This is enhanced by the lack of interruption a retreat setting offers. As we saw in Chapter 4, one aspect of the potency of retreat experiences lies in the relative ease with which unexpected and sometimes unwelcome sensory aberrations can occur. These are often seen as a further tool for the steadying of awareness – provided they can themselves become an object of awareness no different from any other.

A key question concerning the value of mindfulness retreats concerns how far they enable states of mind to be experienced that would be unattainable otherwise. There are conflicting views on this. A supremely articulate spokesperson for the retreat camp is B. Alan Wallace, a physicist, who has spent many years in meditation, often under austere conditions. Wallace (2006) sees meditation as a linear path toward higher states of consciousness, for which a training no less arduous than that of an Olympic athlete is likely to be required. He follows a classification of stages toward attentional balance in which ten levels are identified, divided into three phases.

In the first phase, outward attention is refined in its continuity and its quality. In the second, a taming and pacification of the attention accompanies it being turned inward. In the third, object-less awareness of awareness is cultivated until the goal, the completely balanced state of *shamatha*, is attained. Wallace suggests that a different meditative practice is optimal, but not essential, during each of these stages. Through the first four stages that make up phase one, he proposes that this is practice of mindfulness, as mindfulness of breathing. There should be a progression through these first four steps as a specific aspect is mastered in each. In the first step, proficiency is developed in directing the attention for very short periods. In the second, capacity to maintain attention in the face of distraction improves. During the third, attention becomes more vivid, as skills are acquired in maintaining an equilibrium between lethargy and excitation within focused attention. And in the fourth step, awareness of the breathing becomes much more subtle, as attention to it becomes increasingly close.

Wallace feels it is extremely unlikely that even the third step here can be mastered without experience of meditating in a retreat setting. When he comes to the fourth step, it is assumed this is the context in which students are applying themselves. Wallace therefore provides an especially clear rationale for the intensification of practice during retreats. However, he also feels obliged to point out where and how his concept of 'mindfulness' differs from the one that is most prevalent in the West (and in this book):

The modern Vipassana (contemplative insight) tradition of Theravada Buddhism differs significantly from the Indo-Tibetan Buddhist version [of mindfulness]. The modern Vipassana approach views mindfulness as nondiscriminating, moment-to-moment 'bare awareness'; the Indo-Tibetan tradition, however, characterizes mindfulness as bearing in mind the object of attention, the state of not forgetting, not being distracted, and not floating.

(Wallace 2006: 60)

In the terms favoured by most classifiers of meditation (Goleman 1988; Sole-Leris 1992), it seems that Wallace is identifying mindfulness practice with 'concentration' rather than 'insight'. As traditional teaching on insight meditations has suggested that they can be taken up once a relatively rudimentary level of concentration has been attained, the same link between intensity of practice and experience of retreat settings may not apply. Speculation on such lines can find some support in the relative inexperience of the Asian mindfulness adepts discussed in Chapter 2 (Brown and Engler 1986). Whatever their potential, retreats are felt to be challenging. In practice, they generate a good deal of fear and resistance – before the event and during it. They certainly generate mixed attitudes among mindfulness teachers. Many feel they are especially helpful in accelerating development. Others can voice some suspicion of how far they truly offer something that cannot be obtained through regular practice of the right kind, perhaps seeing them as an unnecessary separation from family, and even a 'retreat' from the most important challenges to becoming and remaining mindful.

Within the retreat environment, the psychological impact of the sustained attention it fosters can be troubling. We saw examples of unusual sensory phenomena arising in this way in Chapter 2, but the manifestations seem most likely to be cognitive, emotional or physical (VanderKooi 1997). At the same time, as some focus group participants mentioned, ordinary actions and responses become more difficult to carry out or feel inaccessible, compounding a feeling of disorientation. Such changes are disturbing when there is a reaction to them, although a concomitant capacity to tolerate and even welcome novel experiences is usually reported. Faith in the power of retreats to intensify meditative experience is confined neither to mindfulness practitioners nor to students of

Wallace's method. One of the qualifications shared by all the members of the supermeditators group in Lutz' study of brain gamma activity (cf. Chapter 2, p. 26) was that they had all been on at least one 3-year-long retreat.

There is much scope for experiment when assessing the extent to which retreats represent a unique opportunity, and if they do, how they might be optimally organised. In terms of mindfulness practice, no comparative data are available concerning, say, the impact of a course of training within a 10-day retreat and the equivalent amount of practice undertaken in classes during an 8-week, part-time course interspersed with daily personal practice. However, the elements of sleep cycle, diet, type of practice, continuity, abstinence from other activities, and teaching are all intermingled and would need to be better distinguished. The development of mindfulness training retreats, designed to meet the needs of professionals wishing to offer mindfulness as an intervention for others, has led to retreats with a wider menu of activities (a dilution of traditional abstinence) and distinctive teaching that does not centre on traditional Buddhist teaching. A comparative evaluation of the impact of modern and traditional retreats on participants' mindfulness would be very revealing, not least in offering a means of assessing the contributions of teaching, through differences in what (Shauna) Shapiro and colleagues (2006) term 'intention' and 'attitude', to the quality of awareness that follows.

Widening the spectrum of mindful practices: the example of poetry

In setting out some of the most common ways in which mindfulness is cultivated, it was implied these were not exhaustive. How might the repertoire of methods be extended? Answers seem most likely to be forthcoming by considering the innate qualities of awareness rather than theoretical deduction. One of these particular qualities seems to be a sensitivity to resonance – how concerted activity in one mind can sympathetically elicit a similar sort of activity in a neighbouring one simply by proximity. This kind of action, as well as underlying the claims for embodiment in the transmission of MBSR to enhance its transmission by example, underpins the capacity of some poetry to modify awareness, something that has also been incorporated into teaching MBSR and MBCT with clinical populations.

Mindful reading often takes the form of reading poetry. The regular use of poetry is one of the striking features of the practice of MBSR that can be inadequately conveyed in written accounts. Selected poems are read (preferably recited) to students in the course of classes, once an initial receptivity has been established. Two poems are especially popular in this context. One is 'The Guest House':

The Guest House

This being human is a guest house.
Every morning a new arrival

A joy, a depression, a meanness,
some momentary awareness comes
as an unexpected visitor.

Welcome and entertain them all!
Even if they're a crowd of sorrows,
who violently sweep your house
empty of its furniture,

still, treat each guest honorably.
He may be clearing you out
for some new delight.

The dark thought, the shame, the malice,
meet them at the door laughing,
and invite them in.

Be grateful for whoever comes,
because each has been sent
as a guide from beyond.
           (Rumi, trans. Coleman Barks; 1994)

The poem is taken from the fifth book of Rumi's six-volume mystical epic, the *Mathnawi*. It is clearly prescriptive, and conveys a morality by which we should not only tolerate but also honour whatever life brings. The unexpected and the sorrowful have a purpose, a role in our development as a 'guide from beyond', even if this is not apparent. At the same time, there is an affirmation that a constant stream of new experience assails us, each a 'momentary awareness'. The poem's advice dwells exclusively on experiences that are 'a crowd of sorrows', but with an injunction to respond to them by acceptance ('welcome and entertain them all'; 'invite them in'), without getting dragged down by them ('meet them at the door laughing'). One assumes the same would apply to the expected or the positively joyous visitor, with the poem encapsulating the virtues of staying equally receptive and tolerant of all experience in a memorable and inspiring way.

Although Rumi has many translators, the verse seems always to be used in Coleman Barks' version in the context of mindfulness training. This is an extremely free and much condensed reading that has been very carefully shaped as a poem in its own right. A fuller and more literal translation (Helminski 2000: 187–8) shows a number of divergences. It is the body that is a guest house and the heart where thoughts 'from the invisible world' are registered. They are not only registered, but, in being honoured, are also retained; for example, 'My soul, regard each thought as a person, for every person's value is in the thought they hold.' Whereas Barks implies that the arrivals include 'a joy' as well as 'a depression, a meanness', Helminski's guests are pure sorrow. Indeed, the poem becomes one about the cleansing power of sorrow as it 'furiously sweeps your house clean'. There are many active metaphors to drive this home – leaves being cleared from the bough of the heart to allow fresher ones to grow; pulling up rotten roots that were hidden from sight so something better can take their place. It is sorrow alone that is 'the servant of the intuitive'. Its grey presence is also protective, in the way that 'frowning clouds' prevent burning by the 'smiling sun'. (This appeal to reason, to strike a calculating balance, is perhaps wisely omitted altogether in Barks' version.) Without venturing into the cosmological implications of references to the source and astrological correspondences that are also absent from Coleman Barks' version, this alternative translation opens up intriguing ambiguities in the basic drift of this widely used poem.

Another favourite is 'Wild Geese':

Wild Geese

You do not have to be good.
You do not have to walk on your knees

for a hundred miles through the desert, repenting.
You only have to let the soft animal of your body love what it
loves.
Tell me about despair, yours, and I will tell you mine.
Meanwhile the world goes on.
Meanwhile the sun and the clear pebbles of the rain
are moving across the landscapes,
over the prairies and the deep trees,
the mountains and the rivers.
Meanwhile the wild geese, high in the clean blue air,
are heading home again.
Whoever you are, no matter how lonely,
the world offers itself to your imagination,
calls to you like the wild geese, harsh and exciting –
over and over announcing your place
in the family of things.

Mary Oliver (Oliver 1986: 14)

While the poems of Rumi have been widely read among people with overtly spiritual inclinations, the work of Mary Oliver enjoys an even wider constituency. She is a hugely successful poet who has earned popular and literary acclaim. It was fitting that a poem by Oliver formed the preface to the most successful new poetry anthology of recent years, *Staying Alive* (Astley 2002). The poem that was chosen was 'Wild Geese'. In some ways, Oliver's verse is the antithesis of the religiose Rumi. Within this poem, 'being good' and going through the most bizarre contortions in the name of 'repentance' crisply sum up the psychological legacy of religion for many people. The poem also conjures up a sense of innate warmth and the simplicity of emotional truthfulness in the two lines that follow. Afterward, the reiterations of 'meanwhile' are a reminder of the independence of nature, amplified by the vastness of the references to prairies, deep trees, mountains and rivers. Connection is re-established through the geese of the title, whose call is not soft – or intelligible – but 'harsh and exciting'. There is some restoration, not to the family at the kitchen table, nor to religion's family of man, but to the broad yet homely 'family of things'. In so far as the poem still attracts a slightly sentimental and cloying quality, it is through anthropomorphism as in the geese 'heading home again'. If 'Wild Geese' lacks the absolute impersonality and mirror finish of a successful haiku, its descriptive language has remained sparse, with details left to the reader's imagination. There is a baring of attention as, like the 'sun and the clear pebbles of the rain', it moves across landscapes taking us with it. As well as conveying a sense of hugeness and hope, the poem is a direct demonstration of a clear, present awareness.

It, too, can therefore help to depict qualities that are sought in the practice of mindfulness. And its simple directness early on, implying that striving too hard can be a long step in the wrong direction, cleverly identifies a trap earnest Westerners face in taking up mindfulness as a practice or discipline invested with a whole new set of 'shoulds'.

Poetry has assumed a place in mindfulness training that no other arts, whether visual, musical or performance, have enjoyed. There is a concentration of meaning in poetry, but also an engagement with words on a physical and bodily level, that is unique to it. Some works, such as David Whyte's *Enough* (Whyte 1990), even make a direct parallel between engagement in poetic and meditative practices.

In a helpful commentary, Shauna Shapiro (2001) reflects on how, as an object for attention, poetry 'appeared to provide students with an alternative route to learning, allowing them to feel, listen and discover in different ways'. In offering a description of her flexible use of poetry to underline the dominant themes of sessions during a mindfulness course, she addresses her readers in similar terms to her students: 'Since each poem affects individuals differently, in reading on, I invite you to notice the effect of the excerpted phrases on your own body, emotions, heart, and mind. Notice what arises and see if you can simply observe each response with nonjudgmental compassion' (Shapiro 2001: 505). This broad conception of the use of poetry as a distillation of experience comes close to Jon Kabat-Zinn's (2005) comments on the primacy of poetry in the context of mindfulness training. In this, he draws a parallel between great poets, yogis and teachers of meditation based on 'deep interior explorations of the mind and of words and of the intimate relationship between inner and outer landscapes'. Poetry therefore possesses 'the potential to enhance our seeing . . . and our ability to feel the poignancy and relevance of our own situations, our own psyches, and our own lives, in ways that help us to understand where the meditation practice may be asking us to look and to see . . . what it is making possible for us to feel and to know'. Kabat-Zinn describes poems as providing fresh lenses for seeing ourselves 'across the span of cultures and of time, offering something more fundamental, something more human than the expected or the already known' (Kabat-Zinn 2005: 27).

Poetry's potential role as an aid in mindfulness training seems multifarious. Poems can be didactic in illustrating an attitude of even-handedness or acceptance that is difficult to communicate by strict definition. They can also serve as particularly fruitful objects for mindful contemplation, by virtue of the combinations of sensation, feeling and thought that they inspire. Yet, in practice, only a tiny minority of published poems are adopted for mindful reading. As in the examples above, these have tended to lack very pronounced metre or rhyme and to be vernacular in their tone, and translations as well as late twentieth-century writers have been favoured. Beyond this, poems seem to be selected only if their substance is overtly compatible with a kindly, meditative outlook. This has tended to be overlooked when comments about the use of poems in mindfulness training are generalised to the whole of poetry. But perhaps the range might be wider, and an apparent fear of non-free verse overcome, if Kabat-Zinn's hope that the spans of time as well as culture be bridged is realised. Is any poem more steeped in mindfulness than this one by Shakespeare?

> Where the bee sucks, there suck I:
> In a cowslip's bell I lie;
> There I couch when owls do cry.
> On the bat's back I do fly
> After summer merrily,
> Merrily, merrily shall I live now
> Under the blossom that hangs on the bough.
> Merrily, merrily shall I live now
> Under the blossom that hangs on the bough.
>   Shakespeare, *The Tempest*, Act V, scene i.

There are many ways in which poetry can seem privileged in its relationship to mindfulness. Kabat-Zinn might have added that poetry is felt by many to have a special integrity among art forms because it is the least likely to lead to either wealth or celebrity. It is hard to be engaged with it without being driven by passion and inner need, rather than possible gains. However, poetry is not necessarily unique, either in the way it introduces a deep resonance that helps hearers become aware in a different way of the reality in and around them, or in the way it provides a direct and extra-ordinarily compact taste of somebody else's world.

For some people, the latter effect is heightened if a poem is set to music in a way that reflects its underlying sensibility. The former effect is something that people can experience if they absorb themselves in the space of particular buildings or other artistic manifestations of frozen form such as sculpture – the impermanent kind as well as the enduring. Here, music has a distinct and vast potential, one that is exploited in the use of bells and chanting in Eastern monastic practices. The ability of bells to impact on other aspects of awareness, long after their sound can no longer be heard, is also called on whenever they are used to signal the start or conclusion of meditation sessions. Related phenomena are described by musically sensitive people, at the conclusion of a piece of music, in terms of an aftertaste as the music literally continues to penetrate and inhabit parts of the mind that few other experiences seem to touch. (In the music systems of India, in which there is a particularly sophisticated understanding of the interconnections between musical form and subtle psychological states, the way in which each *raga* or scale system is associated with its characteristic feeling is spoken of in terms of taste or *rasa*.) This is far from exhausting music's capacity to support mindfulness. Among the members of the focus group reported in Chapter 2, one experienced practitioner had described the importance of musical improvisation in mindful action. Someone with less experience of mindfulness talked with great appreciation of how the discipline of musical practice had brought a focusing of attention along with a sense of internal connectedness. Listening with awareness can initiate a change in consciousness – simply observe the stillness and respira-tion of someone at a concert who is attentively engaged with what they are hearing.

The relative neglect of music among currently favoured ways of developing mindfulness appears to be a historical accident rather than a necessity. The potential of other art forms, too, to foster mindful awareness seems to be underdeveloped. The practical importance of this is that not every mindfulness teacher seems to be equally comfortable in the use of poetry in classes, nor every student equally responsive to it. Perhaps the same flexibility that is often brought to the choice of meditative or directed exercises to foster mindfulness could be brought to the introduction of different art forms.

Special applications

Some adaptations that have been made to adapt mindfulness techniques for adults whose psychological disabilities could compromise their ability to use them were described in Chapter 4. Other accommodations are likely to be needed to take account of groups of people who differ in other ways. The very young and the very old are clear examples of this.

Semple *et al.* (2006) describe how the format of MBCT can be adapted to hold the interest of young children. Parents are actively involved throughout, attending a preliminary session in which they learn the basic techniques that their child will be taught. They receive information too about the entire programme session by session so that they can offer support as co-facilitators. They are also invited to a post-course review session, in which ways in which they can continue to support their child are discussed (Semple *et al.* 2006). Parents do not usually attend the group sessions, which are held for 6–8 children over 12 weeks for no more than 90 minutes at a time. Care is taken to demonstrate that this is not an extension of what they do at home or at school. Children and instructors always sit on the floor, using cushions as well as mats as necessary. As with adult MBCT, exercises are interspersed with discussion sessions, but mindfulness exercises are more varied as well as sometimes being very active. Time for drawing, writing games and stories can also be included. Meditations themselves may not be attempted for more than 5 minutes at a time with frequent changes between activities. These are calculated to involve as many sensory modalities as possible, including sound (with the aid of music), taste and smell. Discussion periods are prefaced by written rules about treating others with care and kindness and asking to speak before doing so. Talking is discouraged during exercises by a written rule of this kind, while one child at any one time can opt out of an activity by sitting in a designated chair. Throughout, the home practice exercises and achievements in the session are rewarded and reinforced with cartoon stickers. The children keep a portfolio of summaries, worksheets, poems and stories as well as the drawings and writings they produce in their own course notebook.

Working with elderly people can present quite different challenges. While their maturity and relative stillness of mind can make them particularly receptive to mindfulness-based approaches, age-related infirmities can interfere with attempts to provide them by a traditional format (Smith 2006). The experience of Smith and others with this population suggests that sessions are best kept short, and particular attention should be paid to cognitive capacities when screening people for the course. Physical infirmities are likely to require sensitive modification of stretching exercises, while walking meditation poses a unique challenge. Although it is normally an opportunity to practise mindfulness of the body in the course of very slow and deliberate movements, paying attention to the parts of the body in the process of walking increases the risk of falls, as it becomes destabilising in the elderly. It is therefore important to restrict instructions to being mindful of being present in their surroundings, in order to avoid such consequences.

Quiet therapy

Mindfulness might be harnessed in the deliberate resolution of a psychological problem, but without any of the discussion that would make the intervention a talking therapy. An interesting set of techniques for this, which he has derived from his reading of Krishnamurti, are described by Robert Cloninger (2004: 84–94). These call forward a state of mindful awareness in the consulting room, in which patients loosen their resistances and silently reacquaint themselves with fended-off experience, without being placed under any pressure to express or verbally reflect upon these. There is an initial phase in which a sense of being calm and awake is encouraged by guidance through a sequence of deep breathing, focusing on the top of the head, and on a positive experience. Cloninger's instructions emphasise acceptance of what is already here, and how the client is, without the wish to become something else.

After 5 minutes, Cloninger moves to the stage he terms 'mindfulness'. Here observation of the emergence of thoughts, as well as letting them go, is paramount. There is an impartial observation of the causes and effects of a thought as it comes into awareness, with a 'metacognitive' awareness of motivation that is a kind of understanding without being a rationalisation or commentary. If a thought is problematic, it is given precedence. All it attaches to is encouraged to surface, without pressure to comment. There is a bringing into presence of the subconscious mind, which Cloninger refers to as 'centering'. This state is held for around 15 minutes. The stage of mindfulness then moves into a final, 'contemplative' one in which a kind of non-dual awareness is sought. Here, after the mind has grown very quiet, the psyche is addressed by the client with a request for help in deepening self-understanding. There is an enlargement of awareness while the client is encouraged not to demand or expect any results. Silence is maintained as an experience of resolution and unity develops.

Cloninger reports that this can lead to removal of the distinction between subject and object. There is a complete and instantaneous understanding of the interdependence of thinking and feeling such that they stop, and the mind (and the brain) becomes very quiet. It is a state of being that is also frictionless because there is no longer internal opposition between parts of the mind that attempt to give direction to others. Like Krishnamurti, he sees this stilling as a natural process, even if it goes against the grain of all habitual mental activity. The entire guided exercise takes no more than 30 minutes.

There is quite a paradox in this procedure as an active application of Krishnamurti's principles. Although Krishnamurti sometimes called the process of understanding the mind 'meditation', he seemed to mean the antithesis of what everybody else refers to as meditation. According to Krishnamurti, meditative practices are ways of dulling the mind rather than liberating it: 'A well disciplined mind is not a free mind, and it is only in freedom that any discoveries can be made'; 'Through self-discipline the mind can strengthen itself in its purpose; but this purpose is self-projected and so it is not the real' (Krishnamurti 1988: 68). For him, meditation was not a discipline of any kind, but what remained when all striving ceased: 'Silence of the mind cannot be brought about through the action of will. There is silence when will ceases. This is meditation' (Krishnamurti 1986: 167). Perhaps the active role of the therapist in Cloninger's procedure, orchestrating the client's process of internal recollection, takes the process closer to Krishnamurti's idea in so far as it attenuates the impact of the client's own intentionality. It seems an intriguing development. This quiet therapy is neither quite meditation nor therapy. Yet, it harnesses something that resembles mindfulness in its effects.

This return to therapy may be the right moment to make an important general but practical point. Working with mindfulness is different from any other health technology, because of what it is as an attentional discipline and the kind of involvement it requires from practitioner and patient. A corollary of this is that both parties are likely to be opening in other ways at the same time as dealing with the kind of mental formations that are recognised by traditional psychopathology. These further developments may not be the point of the intervention, and they might have been achieved in other ways, but they need to be recognised.

Identifying clinical needs

We have referred several times to the importance of choice and of matching the practice to the individual. While this could be seen as a fetish from an over-instrumental approach to mindfulness – one that sees practices as technologies rather than ways of being – the art of matching a meditative method to a student's needs and temperament is explored in classic manuals such as the *Visuddhi-magga* (Buddhaghosa 1999). Harnessing mindfulness at an individual level is likely to be assisted by an updated system of formulation of the factors that are likely to assist such choices. In the field of psychotherapy, there is widespread agreement on the desirability of having some basis on which to formulate someone's capacities and requirements, but rather less consensus on how this is to be done (Johnstone and Dallos 2006). However, if we take the findings from the previous three chapters into account, it is perhaps possible to list the factors that a mindfulness formulation might take into account. These need to include psychological capabilities that indicate the kind of methods someone is most likely to respond to, as well as factors that assist in the diagnosis and delineation of key areas of blockage and difficulty that are likely to be amenable to a mindfulness-based approach. By deliberately restricting the list to 12 candidates, six cognitive abilities and six psychological attributes, the following factors have recommended themselves as being distinct from one another, as having widespread currency, and as being relevant in the context of diagnosable mental health problems:

Factors to consider in case formulation

Concentration (capacity to sustain attention)
Receptiveness (openness and freshness of attention)
Somatic awareness (sensitivity to somatic sensations)
Visualisation (capacity to generate internal images)
Cognitive identification (capacity to relate to thoughts as thoughts)
Recollection (vividness and availability of past memories)

Internal coherence (sense of personal continuity and agency)
Emotional modulation (awareness, tolerance and self-regulation of feelings)
Empathy (ability to enter into others' feelings and viewpoint)
Warmth (capacity to demonstrate love and affection)
Self-attack (tendency to judge, criticise or punish oneself)
Purposefulness (sense of ultimate goals and capacity to generate new meanings)

While there are other cognitive and psychological factors that could be added to a list of this kind, they are unlikely to be independent of these 12 in practice. For instance, emotional range (the breadth of people's emotional experience) will be closely related to their capacity to be aware of feelings. Other factors may be important within other formulation systems, such as verbal intelligence or the capacity to symbolise. They are simply less relevant to choosing between methods where mindfulness-based interventions are concerned.

The aim is not to be exhaustive, and this is all too easily achieved by endless splitting and multiplication of elements, but to have a system whose structure is simple and self-explanatory, and that directly meets the needs of therapists and prospective clients. In a similar spirit, the components of the formulation would be qualities that can be recognised from a face-to-face meeting without recourse to distracting tests and inventories, with sensitivity to them deepening with practice. Use of them should develop and organise observations that a therapist naturally values and makes instinctively. The results can be discussed openly with clients in order to arrive at an agreement of where they currently stand. This provisional schema needs to be fully tested out in practice before it is used in a prescriptive way. Each component's inclusion will be justified by its usefulness when shaping plans for interventions that are likely to be beneficial for a given client or patient.

Example

Josie, a teacher in her early forties, has been seeking help since she was suddenly left by her husband four months before. She has no history of frank psychiatric illness or use of meditative techniques. She used cannabis intermittently in adolescence and at college and describes lifelong self-doubt and a pattern of living through her husband and his friends' wives. She had been unable to conceive with him, and, while he had tried to reassure her that this did not matter, he has now set up home with a younger woman. She has felt she is falling apart and is kept awake by nightmares in which she experiences herself as having a miscarriage of a fully formed foetus without anybody there to help her, after which she cannot stop bleeding. She finds it difficult to notice the weather or to taste the coffee she is drinking. She hates being alone and is constantly phoning up their friends. She feels she is alienating them with her crying, remonstrations and questions. She switches between believing that her husband is a demon that she should be revenged upon, and feeling that she is a useless, unattractive bore whom anybody would be better off without.

What is very distinctive about the phenomenology here is the profusion of affects (anger, self-hate, guilt and sadness), far from fully felt, alongside evidence that these are poorly modulated. Affective changes are associated with discontinuities in Josie's sense of herself, while she attacks herself psychologically even if there is no frank physical self-harm. (The specificity of her recollections may be a relevant and positive prognostic sign here.) Experiences from which she is emotionally cut off seem more accessible to her through visualisation than from awareness of what is happening in her body.

A number of different treatment approaches for Josie are possible. The analysis here is likely to be helpful when considering mindfulness-based ones. Josie would be likely to find the full force of her feelings overwhelming if they were to be suddenly released. A recommendation for her to face them in a more modulated way would emphasise a gradual introduction to somatic focusing, first as a way of being able to ground herself away from the maelstrom of what is rushing through her head, and then to build up some attentional stability. Once there is a capacity to give attention to ordinary sensations and to experience these relatively fully, consideration could be given to moving attention to her thoughts and feelings so that these are experienced in themselves, instead of a chaotic confusion. Ultimately, being able to decentre from the very rigid either/or thinking that accompanies her sudden mood changes is likely to be of considerable help in finding ways to disengage from them. None of this would be a substitute for a working relationship with someone who is simultaneously and empathically able to help her explore and articulate what is happening at each step. However, judicious introduction of attentional practices in this way seems likely to facilitate and hasten a healing process.

In this instance, formulation is being used to design an individualised treatment. It suggests components it might include (and avoid) as well as highlighting likely areas of difficulty. Some other instances of how mindfulness techniques can be chosen and incorporated within individualised treatments are provided by Germer (2005a). When choices are being made between complete packages such as DBT or ACT, much can depend upon the components that accompany the mindfulness training they offer. They cannot be considered solely in terms of their approach to mindfulness. DBT may be indicated not only by the brevity of patients' attention span, but also by the prominence of their self-destructive behaviour. Patients likely to benefit from DBT's explanations and contained guidance may find, say, ACT's radical questioning of underlying goals too challenging until they have achieved greater internal stability.

Integrating mindfulness within the clinical setting

Harnessing mindfulness is not only a matter of being able to introduce it and having an appropriate set of tools to offer. In clinical practice, it has to be introduced into a setting whose impact is likely to be critical in either supporting or undermining what is taught.

The development of MCBT as a specific treatment for depression that can be learned and used by mental health professionals is a hugely significant development in bringing mindfulness into routine mental health practice. Earlier chapters have illustrated how MBCT and the MBSR programme can be adapted to meet the needs of people diagnosed with individual disorders. In generic community mental health practice, these diagnoses may be less clear-cut, and the client population quite mixed in the spread of the difficulties they represent. Prospective participants are also relatively vulnerable, and examples have been given already of how and when untimely attempts to engage in mindfulness practice can worsen their difficulties or bring additional problems. In order to present an 8-week training package to a mixed group of mental health service attenders, two issues that have to be confronted straightaway are assessment of potential group members and the working format of the groups.

The traditional assessment model for the MBSR outpatient programme in physical health settings has been an opt-in model (cf. Chapter 3, p. 59). Potential participants for a course are identified and are invited to attend an introductory seminar in which the principles of mindfulness practice, the nature of the course, and the likely gains and pains are set out. Any screening and exclusion of individuals on the basis of suspected inability to benefit or potential disruption to the class has ordinarily taken place by this stage through the information provided by referrers, possibly with the addition of prospective clients' responses to preliminary questionnaires. They are invited to make a choice, based on this experience, whether they wish to continue, the course being likely to follow in subsequent weeks. These sessions are potentially helpful for instructors to get a sense of the overall balance of a new group before it begins, its strengths and potential sticking points.

In running a group with users of mental health services, it is very unlikely that the large groups of over 30 individuals (plus trainees and other visitors) often found in MBSR practice in general hospitals would be appropriate. Many people with mental health problems are very wary of others, and of others' reactions to them, in ways that make coming to a group with strangers, and undertaking and talking about challenging new experiences in front of them, much more threatening than they would be otherwise. In addition, there will be some tension between the principles of an adult learning or coaching model, in which professionals make themselves available to develop skills in the service of a client's life choices, and the formal duties of care under which mental health professionals ordinarily work. These bring a need to be highly attentive to changes in patients' mental health, and a readiness to take additional action where there is justifiable concern about an individual. In effect, this is likely to mean that mindfulness teachers have to be able to pay attention to each individual within the group and to think systematically about each individual, whether or not in attendance, for each week of the programme.

Careful thought needs to be given to both the overall size of the group and to how the format is modified within sessions to reduce feelings of pressure. Although didactic phases, in which techniques are introduced, poems read, or homework set, may be delivered to the entire group, phases in which exploration and disclosure are required, as when experiences of exercises and the findings from homework are discussed, may be better met by dividing the group. Initial discussions of reactions to new material might be in private pairs rather than before the whole group. When the instructors' input is essential, the group may divide, with one instructor per subgroup. With time, as confidence in discussion grows, the group can take on more of the character of a therapeutic group, with members learning directly from the experience of anyone else present.

The development of courses in either community or inpatient settings is greatly facilitated if the staff responsible can establish a group of their own. This allows coming together for a shared experience of mindfulness (through a shared meditation or exercise) as well as an opportunity to share and learn from experiences in the patient groups. In this, as in the concerted work to maintain a working group format in the sessions for service attenders, there is exploitation of the principle of resonance, by which mindfulness is enhanced by others' participation and proximity.

Meeting the needs of future professionals

Mindfulness-based interventions have been used successfully with medical students for around 15 years. This reflects the high stress levels these students often exhibit, as well, perhaps, as the considerable consequences that failure on their courses would carry. Despite this, the evaluative literature on these interventions is relatively scant, although a good deal has been learned and reported about effective methods of engaging and teaching this population. Three current models can be briefly contrasted, as practised in Philadelphia, Arizona, and Monash, Australia.

The Philadelphia model

The leaders at Jefferson Medical College are Diane Reibel and Steven Rosenzweig. They have used two different models for providing mindfulness training since the late 1990s. At first, the training was an option that students selected from alternatives during regular teaching hours, only a minority taking it up. Subsequently, it has become an out-of-hours option for as many students as wish to come. In either format, it has been closely integrated with formal teaching on the physiology of stress. Three hours of this teaching are provided in the first year of medical training, with an emphasis on the importance of individuals' contributions to experienced stress and on students checking out their own experiences (Rosenzweig 2004). For instance, students might be invited to notice what is going on in their bodies and minds before a slide is introduced with the words, 'any word on the next slide could be on your exam'. They are then invited to relate the sensations going on in their bodies to the picture of the autonomic nervous system that the slide in fact carries. Later, they will be invited to check how they can modify the action of their own autonomic nervous system through breathing exercises. More colourful examples of the extremes of self-regulation are presented prior to an introduction to readily available systems such as biofeedback and autogenic training. Subsequent teaching builds on this to emphasise the serious health consequences of stress and failure to self-regulate, constantly referring to students' existing scientific knowledge.

After stress physiology teaching, those who are interested in learning more self-regulatory techniques are invited to an introductory session, to learn about MBSR. Following a specimen led meditation, a 6-week 'elective' training is offered to volunteers. It appears that this is best timed early in the students' studies, but after they have had some opportunity to experience the stresses of this new role. These come from several sources, social as well as academic (financial stress from debt, the loss of free time, and disconnection from family, as well as the existential challenge of facing death in the course of medical work). Reibel and

Rosenzweig have also referred to the spiritual challenge of life being demystified through a relentless induction into reductionist thinking. On top of all this comes the personal psychological challenge of enduring sleeplessness alongside a relative absence of social support, something that may be exacerbated as traditional mechanisms for peer support within the medical community have been eroded.

MBSR was therefore conceived as a way of improving personal wellness in the face of these challenges, as well as a means of developing or preserving compassion in the face of demands either to close down emotionally, or be overwhelmed by patients' difficulties. Learning to follow an explicit path of compassion through such training was seen as a middle way that could be bearable, without compromising personal sensitivity. It also brought wider benefits because it relied on students learning how to teach useful techniques to their patients.

In practice, the student courses are very similar to MBSR as taught in other settings. The foundational practices from MBSR programmes are included, such as sitting meditations, body scan, walking meditation and guided yoga. The personal wellness theme is introduced with a 'well meditation', in which participants are invited to be as authentic as possible and to acknowledge their reasons for coming. Information on relevant scientific papers is provided, while students are reminded that the class will not be about these, depending instead on direct experience. Overall, the curriculum is skeletal and flexible, providing a counterweight to the over-organisation and indigestibility of other classes the students encounter. The leader reassures them that the rate and order of presentation will depend upon what is happening in the class and requests a commitment to regular practice between sessions. This is usually 20 minutes per day, assisted by prerecorded practice tapes.

Given students' tendency to live and suffer in their heads, Rosenzweig and Reibel have found it very important to use physical movement in classes with this group – starting every class with this in different forms. Medical students tend to be very competitive and self-sufficient; sharing experiences in group discussions can be much harder for them than for other groups. Little sharing is required to begin with, with the introduction of 'mindful listening', practised in pairs at first. A distinctive part of the content of the student mindfulness curriculum is practice in silently cultivating wholesome states through specific meditations. In this way, compassion, loving kindness, and joy are experienced with encouragement that these can be made available for others. This is emphasised in discussion of what to do when apparently nothing more can be done for a patient. This seems to be an especially valued aspect of the instruction.

The Philadelphia team have performed detailed evaluations of the impact of MBSR with a heterogeneous sample of 136 general hospital patients (Reibel *et al.* 2001) as well as a non-randomised but comparative evaluation of 140 second-year students opting to have classes in MBSR, compared with 162 students opting to have classes in complementary medicine (Rosenzweig *et al.* 2003). Their approach to assessment of the impact of the intervention was quite different in the two populations. Observations of the students were confined to changes in total mood disturbance, using a little used 'profile of mood states'. Although mood disturbance was significantly greater among the self-selected cohort going through MBSR at the study's outset, their scores showed a significant decrease, while the control subjects showed an even greater increase in mood disturbance over the same 10-week interval.

The Arizona programme

This is very closely linked to the MBSR model. The main amendment is a greater emphasis on cultivation of positive affect, through inclusion of specific exercises to engender feelings of loving kindness and forgiveness and the cultivation of empathy skills in the course of small group discussions. This reflects a rethinking of the qualities of mindfulness, which effectively provide the curriculum for the training. Jon Kabat-Zinn (1990: 33–40) had identified seven attitudinal foundations of mindfulness:

1   non-judging (not evaluating or categorising)
2   patience (letting things unfold in their own time)
3   beginner's mind (being willing to see anything afresh)
4   trust (of oneself, of one's experience and of life)
5   non-striving (not trying to get to a goal or outcome)
6   acceptance (seeing things as they actually are in the present)
7   letting go (allowing thoughts, feelings, etc., to pass away).

To which Shapiro and colleagues have added these five (Shapiro and Schwarz 1999):

1   gentleness (being soft, considerate and tender)
2   generosity (giving without thought of return)
3   empathy (feeling for and understanding others in the present)
4   gratitude (reverence and appreciation for what is present)
5   loving kindness (unconditional benevolence and love).

This means that, even more explicitly than in the Philadelphia courses, fundamental attitudes of warmth, giving and self-negation are fostered, together with compassion and forgiveness (which Shapiro and Schwarz see as part of loving kindness). Apart from benefits in terms of personal stress and coping, the course is intended to touch core professional values.

This programme is distinguished by being the subject of the only truly randomised comparative evaluation to date (Shapiro *et al.* 1998). An initial cohort of 200 students from more than one year (medical and premedical) were given the opportunity to participate, knowing they would be randomised between an intervention group and a 'wait-list' control. This produced 78 consenting participants, whose 'random' allocation was still stratified for gender, race and course year. The 37 students who received the intervention did so in two classes, each with a different instructor. The classes met over 8 weeks, the sequence of exercises closely following Kabat-Zinn (1990), with a strong emphasis on group discussion. Evaluation compared immediate post-course scores with precourse scores on measures of anxiety, global psychological distress, empathy and spiritual experiences. The post-course evaluation coincided with a time of high external stress (examinations), when comparisons were also drawn with the wait-list controls. (These were given a brief, one-off meditation class prior to testing to control for any post-session effects on the day of evaluation.) The wait-list controls went on to the intervention themselves, and showed similar positive changes at the end of 8 weeks. All evaluations were administered by an independent experimenter, blind to treatment exposure. The daily practice of participants was monitored to allow analysis of the impact of compliance with the programme.

The study allowed six sets of comparisons, all with significant differences between the pre- and post-intervention scores of the course attendees compared with controls. In three measures, the two groups moved in opposite directions – state anxiety, depression and empathy. In the other three, the controls' scores were virtually static, with the course attendees' scores moving in the expected direction (trait anxiety, general severity index and a measure of 'spirituality'). The pre-post measures were then repeated for the control students who subsequently attended the course. In every case (except trait anxiety, which had to be omitted for operational reasons), the change in scores through the course replicated that of the original attendees. A particularly interesting aspect of the study is the demonstration of at least a short-term impact on the students' empathy (measured using a local version of the Empathy Construct Rating Scale). While the measures of depression and anxiety support a stress-reducing effect, this is indeed evidence of how the training can further the development of core professional attitudes and values.

The Monash model

This Australian model differs significantly from the others here, as it was developed independently of the MBSR tradition. Mindfulness skills are built up progressively from brief meditations to longer exercises, while there is a greater emphasis on simultaneous development of specific cognitive skills that are associated with 'stress release' (Hassed 2004). Introduced in sequence, these comprise perception, acceptance, presence of mind, limitations, listening, self-discipline, emotions, and understanding of 'self-interest'. Classes involve illustration, discussion and exercises focusing on each skill, followed by review the next session. Despite its origins, Hassed's model is not greatly different from 'lite' variations of MBSR that have been provided as introductory training for professional groups within tight time constraints elsewhere. What is unique is its complete integration within the medical school curriculum. It is compulsory for all students, being an integral part of teaching in a 'health enhancement programme' that bases all teaching around a positive conception of health, representing 5 per cent of the total programme (Hassed 2005a). Stress management tutorials and skills training are provided over 6 weeks in the first semester of the first year, with top-ups in later years. Understanding of the principles of 'mindfulness-based stress management' is formally examined by OSCE (objective structured clinical examination) stations.

Hassed has conducted research into the impact of the programme, but without standardised measures or investigation of its relative benefits in relation to specific sources of stress. He has produced data (from a partial sample of volunteers only) on students' actual use of specific coping strategies subsequent to the programme (Hassed 2005b). This shows that, in addition to newly learned meditation and cognitive techniques, students subsequently rely more on healthy nutrition, exercise and social support to manage stress. However, this programme, too, appears to provide an education in professional values that goes well beyond stress reduction.

The fruits of mindfulness: a paradox

For many, the Buddha's words to Bahiya, quoted at the outset of this chapter, are the quintessence of the Buddha's teaching. Shorn of the elaboration and repetition that is so characteristic of the Buddhist scriptures encountered in the first chapter, we are left with a verse to meet the *Dhammapada*'s plea for a 'single verse that brings peace'. When you see, do nothing but see. When you hear, do nothing but hear. For touching, tasting, sensing and cognising, likewise. Are things really so simple? As in so many of the commentaries and *suttas*, the Buddha's reported words come within a context. Moreover, in the telling of this very famous story, it is a context that gets hugely changed in the telling. In all versions, Bahiya is a supplicant who comes to ask the Buddha how he may achieve liberation. When he hears the Buddha's words, the effect is immediate and he achieves enlightenment straightaway. But why is the Buddha's teaching so remarkably direct and so effective in Bahiya's case?

Two elements are usually present in the fuller story. One is that Bahiya is about to die. He knows he is going to die. The Buddha sees he is about to die. There is no time to be lost. Every word, every breath counts. So not a syllable is wasted. And just after his liberation, Bahiya's death comes anyway. The other element is preparation. Bahiya may be presented as somebody who is primed for liberation through his precarnate relationship with the Buddha (as in Burlingame's own account). Or the narrator may stress Bahiya's saintliness achieved through good works and purity of mind (e.g. Hart 1988: 116–17). Sometimes Bahiya's readiness is expressed in terms of having attained the eighth state of concentration, as if the Buddha assisted with a final ineffable nudge that would otherwise have little effect.

Already, there are so many additional things that one should be doing – beyond just seeing – to generate no end of spiritual exertion. And that is assuming that the words actually had meaning to Bahiya as words; that happenings on the cusp of death are relevant to other phases of life; or that the sheer presence of the Buddha might not affect the relationship between mindful effort and awakening. Avid readers of Chapter 1 will recall how the great *sutta* on mindfulness closed with the Buddha radically dropping the threshold at which liberation might be achieved, provided the meditator's inner condition was ripe. In this chapter's discussion of retreats, it was evident that emphasis on patient, slow progress toward desired states of balanced attention was even greater in other schools than for the early Buddhism we have been drawing on here. The story of Bahiya provides enigmatically few answers as to the preparation that is truly required, if any, before untainted seeing, hearing, sensing or cognising becomes possible here and now.

Conclusions

While many methods of cultivating mindfulness are already available, much scope remains for others to be developed. Tracking the internal reverberations from different kinds of aesthetic experience affords just one example. The intensification of mindfulness during residential retreats offers an important opportunity to evaluate the relative contributions of practice, continuity, presence of others and teaching on changes in awareness. Methods of adapting individual techniques to the person can take non-psychological factors into account, including age. The formulation of a person's attentional strengths and blind spots may be helpful in designing treatment plans to address individual clinical needs. Mindfulness can be adapted and taught to mixed groups in mental health settings if appropriate arrangements are made, while their potential use in inpatient settings seems underexplored. Current issues in the training of future professionals in mindfulness are considered in relation to the specific needs of medical students. These have included the refreshment and revitalisation of basic motivations and values, as mindfulness practices are complemented by others designed to cultivate positive affects and compassion.

Chapter 6

Mental health and mindfulness

> The secret of happiness is this: let your interests be as wide as
> possible, and let your reactions to the things and persons that
> interest you be as far as possible friendly rather than hostile.
> Bertrand Russell, *The Conquest of Happiness* (1955: 123)

Does mindfulness inexorably support healthy development? This
might be answered by a consideration of the markers of health,
such as psychological status, adjustment, satisfaction and productivity, of people exhibiting different degrees of attainment. I am
unaware of any study having such breadth, but counter-examples
go a long way to nullify a hypothesis of this kind. While there is
significant scientific and anecdotal evidence of the frequently positive impact of mindfulness on negative moods, tension and intrusive mental events, there is relatively little concerning what many
would feel is a cardinal indicator of health: interpersonal relationships. We shall look first at how mental health can be thought
about as something other than absence of mental illness, giving
priority to models that refer to awareness and attention in developing their alternative concepts of health. These will provide a
useful context in further consideration of where mindfulness stands
in relation to mental health.

Mental health

In Chapter 1, we saw how, in traditional Buddhism, mindfulness
was identified with a unique form of mental purification that not
only overcame sorrow, distress, pain and sadness, but also set the

practitioner on the right path to achieve the permanent liberation represented by *Nibbana*. In Chapter 2, three contrasting types of study conducted with experienced mindfulness practitioners were reported. They were each consistent with mindfulness practice being associated with continuing changes in awareness over time, and with psychological changes taken to signify greater well-being. In Chapter 3, the different aims and methods of some Western therapeutic approaches that embrace mindfulness were outlined. These point to different ways in which it can promote health, through the prevention as well as the alleviation of recognised mental disorders. We also saw how tensions can appear between mindfulness and other aspects of a traditional psychotherapeutic framework if it is introduced. In Chapter 4, the ways in which mindfulness-dependent treatments are used to relieve psychological disorders were reviewed, noting the incompleteness of the evidence at present. Analysis of its likely actions when used therapeutically for specific conditions helps to identify what may be crucial to its healing function. In Chapter 5, the foundations or establishings of mindfulness were considered in contemporary terms. It was noted that techniques that have complemented it in traditional settings, such as practices for loving kindness or compassion, are finding contemporary analogues too.

At least two important questions remain for this survey. One, that surfaced more than once in Chapter 4, is the extent to which it is possible to detach mindfulness as something which helps in the treatment of mental disorders from something that contributes to mental health through personal growth and the flourishing of latent capabilities. The other, touched on when investigating the scope of mindfulness in Chapters 1 and 2, is the basis of its contribution to such broader aspects of mental health.

The answers may be less obvious than they first appear. One very distinctive characteristic of mindfulness is its emphasis on process. It begins and ends with awareness, rather than any of the contents of experience. Mindfulness cannot be identified with a particular aim or a particular result. Kabat-Zinn (2005) has summarised this understanding by emphasising how meditation is a way of being, rather than a technique. While it is the nature of mindfulness for awareness to be shared without favour between all things that present to it, he also indicates the importance of being aware in a non-discursive way of factors influencing the unfolding of awareness, and of how these work either to liberate or imprison us at each moment. Because mindfulness is not about getting anything or anywhere special, but accepting how things truly are, the old lyric seems apposite: 'It's not what you do, but the way that you do it.'

In contrast to this focus on process, it is commonly assumed that mental health is dependent on factors such as people's relationships or their sense of meaning and purpose. While these can support the development of mindfulness, and may benefit from it, they are not attentional processes and cannot be identified with mindfulness. An alternative construct that has been recently implicated in discussions of psychological well-being, and that is identified with attentional process, is Csikszentmihalyi's (1990) concept of 'flow'.

Flow and mental health

The concept of flow was refined by close attention to the experience and circumstances of people when they recognise that they are happy. Relative to overtly pleasurable situations such as eating or sex, situations in which people feel challenged yet fully engaged relative to their abilities, and carried along by the activity, are associated with even greater enjoyment. A recent summary helpfully distinguishes between features of 'flow' that characterise it as an experience and those that seem crucial to bringing it about and maintaining it (Nakamura and Csikszentmihalyi 2003). Five intrinsic qualities are described as follows: 1. intense, focused concentration on the here and now; 2. loss of awareness of self alongside absorption in the action; 3. confidence about being able to respond to whatever is required; 4. loss of awareness of time passing; and 5. experiencing the activity as intrinsically worthwhile. (In public lectures, Csikszentmihalyi may also emphasise the subjective serenity that accompanies the loss of awareness of self, and the sense of being outside everyday reality that amounts to ecstasy in its literal sense.) The three aspects Nakamura and Csikszentmihalyi cite as promoting flow during an activity are as follows: 1. remaining clear about immediate goals; 2. receiving continuous and clear feedback about the quality of one's performance; and 3. having opportunities that stretch existing capacities.

There is an emphasis on process here, too, characterised by a particular quality of consciousness. Some of flow's qualities, such as involvement, presentness and clarity, as well as its intrinsic motivation, are shared with mindfulness. Others, such as the transcendence of self and even of reality, are seemingly less so. However, the kind of absorption found in flow is dependent upon having productive activities to be engaged in. It is also associated with achievement, the activities having to offer the right degree of challenge, as well as continual feedback. (It definitely matters what you do here, as well as how you do it.) While many people do experience such flow states regularly, there are considerable differences in the extent to which people experience it in practice. Around 15 per cent of us reportedly never experience it at all. Practically, flow is an invitation to arrange life so that situations are engineered that bring the optimum level of 'challenge' to meet the 'skills' a person has. Too much challenge relative to skill brings the neutrality of 'arousal', leading to overt dysphoria and anxiety where insufficient skill is available. Too little challenge relative to skill, brings first the less satisfying condition of 'control', before relaxation sets in. Where both challenge and skill are lacking, states of apathy that are the antithesis of flow appear.

Although an alteration of consciousness is required, flow is usually brought about by indirect manipulation of factors that stimulate attention, rather than through attending to (or 'paying') attention directly. While its associations with happiness and productivity make flow seem a desirable state to enter, it makes an interesting phenomenon against which notions of mental health can be tested and refined. Is it the state itself or its consequences that are what would be healthy? If the state itself, can something as broad as health be identified with states that are so dependent on conditions, such as participating in activities? If the consequences, are there sequelae to flow experiences that are unique to them, as opposed to a general feeling of satisfaction or happiness? And are there negative sequelae, such as indifference to other things that need attention, or an inability to divide attention, that could seem unhealthy from other perspectives?

Used in this way, the concept of flow reminds us that discussion of health quickly implicates the environment. Indeed, the difficulty of equating health with some fixed mental or bodily state, without considering the need to adapt to a given environment, has been a theme in Western medical philosophy at least since Hippocrates. Modern writers such as Rene Dubois (1966) restored this perspective in modern conceptions of health, and the possibility of

identifying mental health with a balance between self and environment is being developed within the positive psychology movement
by writers like Jonathan Haidt (2006).

Mental health and well-being

Recently, there has been a resurgence of interest in the concept of
well-being, an appealing proxy for that of mental health when
something more than the absence of illness is being referred to.
'Well-being' is suitably upbeat and manages to embrace being well
and feeling well. These are not necessarily the same thing. A tension
between being well and feeling well may go back at least to
Aristotle, who developed a concept of human flourishing, or *eudaemonia*, that involved the realisation of qualities he felt essential to
the human soul. Aristotle's own concern was that a political as well
as a psychological harmony should result, with inner balance
reflecting an outer one. *Eudaemonia* made a good candidate for a
conception of mental health that reflects the importance of environment, at the same time as accepting it could not be equated with
simplistic conceptions of happiness (Nussbaum 1994).

Well-being has been adopted within the positive psychology
movement to help people identify components of how they function that are already 'signature strengths' and others that may
need attention in order to maximise personal well-being (Peterson
and Seligman 2004). Accordingly, those intent on achieving well-
being undergo intensive self-diagnosis, and then sign up to
developing the strengths that are relatively weak through a series
of exercises devised for the purpose. Haidt (2006) has commented
on the confusion that can arise here between 'relentless self-
improvement' and 'authenticity', as well doing may not be the
same as well-being. (In other words, being well may just be being,
period.)

Whatever the precise methods that are employed, an emphasis on
improving well-being, over and above recovery from specific
difficulties, suggests that mental health is likely to lie in the attainment of the good relations and satisfying activities and interests
with which it is ordinarily associated. This involves a kind of
deliberate or assisted reorganisation of one's desires, relationships
and projects, a project closer to moral regeneration than is commonly admitted. A formulation of well-being in terms of character,
value orientation and relationship on the lines that have become

popular among positive psychologists is congruent with the kind of enduring (if recently neglected) ideals in Western culture mentioned in earlier remarks on Aristotle. But it ignores the significance of experiential processes in a way that 'flow' did not. A model that managed to combine both might therefore be more helpful to the present discussion.

Cloninger's model of health and well-being

In recent years, the internationally distinguished psychiatrist Robert Cloninger has used his understanding of psychological potential to produce an unusually comprehensive map of mental health (Cloninger 1999, 2004). It reaches from mental disorders, through a person's capacity to adapt, toward ways of realising latent creative and spiritual capacities. In doing so, Cloninger draws on a good deal of his own work on fundamental facets of personality. Some parts appear to be more crucial to pathological development; others to self-transcendent forms of psychological growth. His work is particularly relevant in relating mindfulness to mental health because he uses degrees of self-awareness as a fundamental dimension along which people can be separated. Some understanding of his work on personality is necessary to present this.

In his studies of personality, Cloninger identified a small number of independent components. These each correspond to behavioural and psychological traits, can be quantified, and can be demonstrated to show independent patterns of heritability and to be associated with specific patterns of brain activation. A first group, comprising four 'temperamental' factors, governs how people interact with stimuli in their environment from birth. These factors underpin many forms of psychopathology, especially those attributed to personality disorder. They are set out in the following box:

Harm avoidance observed as pessimistic worry in anticipation of problems, fear of uncertainty, shyness with strangers, and rapid fatiguability.

Novelty seeking observed as exploratory activity in response to novelty, impulsiveness, extravagance in approach to cues of reward, and active avoidance of frustration

Reward dependence observed as sentimentality, social sensitivity, attachment, and dependence on approval by others

> **Persistence** observed as industriousness, determination, and perfectionism (linked to maintenance of reward dependence when reinforcement is very intermittent).

Cloninger's model is particularly effective at articulating the correspondences and interrelationships between these factors. For instance, it hypothesises that four of the personality disorders that are grouped together because of their instability in the American Psychiatric Association's classification (APA 2004) – histrionic, antisocial, borderline and narcissistic – each differ only in their pronounced novelty seeking from dispositions that are, respectively, reliable, schizoid, obsessional or avoidant. A very broad spectrum of psychopathology is certainly covered.

The second set (see the following box) comprises three 'characterological' factors, each of which is amenable to further development as self-awareness grows.

> **Self-direction** – being responsible, reliable, resourceful, goal-oriented, and self-confident
> **Cooperativeness** – being empathic, tolerant, compassionate, supportive, and principled
> **Self-transcendence** – being spiritual, unpretentious, humble, and fulfilled

Cloninger makes specific analogies between the development of these character traits and aspects of attention that contribute to the general growth of self-awareness. There is what he terms an 'elevation' of awareness, such that it grows in purposive impartiality and recollectability. This is associated with the trait of self-directedness (and medial prefrontal activity). Secondly, there is flexibility in the breadth of attention while maintaining a mobile alertness. This is associated with cooperativeness (and networks for arousal and cooperativeness in the right frontal and inferior parietal cortex and the insula). Third, there is depth of attention, evident in a capacity to attend non-judgementally to meaningful, previously unconscious experience. (He associates this with networks for inhibitory control of conflict and self-transcendence: anterior cingulate, lateral prefrontal cortex and basal ganglia.)

In combination, permutations of the characterological factors lead to different dispositions. An 'organised' state results when self-direction and cooperation are present, without self-transcendence. When self-transcendence is added, a 'creative' disposition emerges. At the opposite pole to this creative state is 'melancholic' (downcast), representing weakness in all three. This opposition between depression and creativity is borne out by Cloninger's empirical research into the correlation of subjective happiness with the presence of these three character traits. This showed that possession of 'self-direction' in particular greatly influences whether a person will feel happy or sad. When self-direction, cooperativeness and self-transcendence are all lacking, the chances of feeling sad are very high indeed (Cloninger *et al.* 1998). Despite the differences in language and approach, there is a striking correspondence between this antithesis between creativity and melancholy, and that between 'flow' and 'apathy' found in Csikszentmihalyi's model (cf. p. 141 above).

In placing experiential processes centre stage, Cloninger identifies three overall levels at which human awareness is organised. The first is established once there is a capacity for identifying volition, feelings and thoughts; the second, mindful, level is established once there is a capacity to be aware of subconscious material and for metacognition (albeit with retention of a sharp duality between the observer and what is observed); the third, contemplative, level is progressively non-dualistic. This means the distinction between observer and observed reduces as perception takes on a trans-personal quality and action is experienced as effortless and free from conflict. In Cloninger's hierarchy of mental functioning, attainment of each successive level is commensurate with greater personal health.

Cloninger's work is audacious in its breadth and combines much more detailed description of the architecture of these levels of awareness than it is appropriate to summarise here (see Cloninger 2004: Chapter 5). He makes important proposals for practical interventions that would make these states more accessible to patients in the consulting room (cf. pp. 123–4 above). Its capacity to link the whole range of health from frank psychopathology to higher potentials deserves anyone's further study. However, when considering mental health in relation to human potential, it was the true apostle of positive psychology, Abraham Maslow, who anticipated the usefulness of a detailed examination of the actual experiences of those people who appeared to be exceptionally healthy for a reappraisal of what it is to be mentally healthy.

Maslow and self-actualisation

Maslow had a lifelong interest in human potential, which he expressed initially in his hierarchical conception of motivation (Maslow 1954). Once basic needs for nutriment, safety, association and esteem are satisfied, others, such as the search for meaning and transcendence, come into play. When he turned his attention to health, Maslow felt it should encompass the whole spectrum of activity. Equating a positive state of health with what he termed self-actualisation, he expected truly healthy people to be relatively free from frank illness; to have satisfied the four kinds of basic needs just listed; and to be demonstrably in tune with themselves through the fulfilment of the other talents and capacities they were born with. He found that people who satisfied these criteria of health were likely to have other characteristics in common, which he summarised in terms of their demonstration of a distinctive form of cognition.

Maslow distinguished between two modes of cognition. Both are based on in-depth interviews with hundreds of subjects, people who had, or had never had, the sort of self-limiting transcendental moments he called 'peak experiences' as well as people whom he saw as 'self-actualising' (Maslow 1954). Because both modes are based on detailed observation, they manage to link subjective experience with psychological generalisation. Maslow terms the first, and most usual, mode of cognition the D mode after 'D' for deficiency. It is commonly encountered among people who are not self-actualised and is fitted to a basic attitude to the world in which lack is ever-present. Maslow (1908–1970) was a close contemporary of Jean-Paul Sartre (1905–1980). There is an extraordinary complementarity between their work that appears not to have been recognised by commentators. Sartre's depiction of the human condition throughout his novels and existential style of philosophising, dominated as it is by a sense of internal lack and a nihilistic attitude to a world whose fundamental characteristic is thought to be scarcity, amounts to a distillation of D cognition. Maslow's D cognition is individualistic and instrumental. Experience is always selective, according to current motivations. Perceptions of the world are precategorised according to our ideas about it. Perceptions of others are filtered according to our apparent needs of them and the uses we have for them. While D cognition can supply plans and projects for managing deficiency, it has no real way of eliminating it.

The other mode of cognition was termed B cognition (for 'being'). According to Maslow, B cognition embraces two distinct if related kinds of apprehension. In one, there is a widening of perception so that the subject is vividly aware of many levels of experience simultaneously. In the other, there is a rapt concentration on one detail that assumes total significance in itself, as many ordinarily unobserved aspects become apparent. What both sorts of apprehension share is a suspension of the sense of self, and of ordinary ideas of time and space, with a sense of unity between everything that is present.

Maslow's ideas remain highly relevant and helpful because of the contrasts between his sketches of the D and B modes. Indeed, it would be possible to take his observations concerning D cognition to outline a psychology of mental ill health in terms of key processes and the experiences associated with them. The various components of D functioning become exaggerated in the psychological functioning associated with the main kinds of mental disorder. For instance, the tendency to see any object as a separate part of the perceptual field extrapolates to the fragmentation of psychotic states; very selective attention is characteristic of emotional and paranoid disorders; taking repeated comparisons to extremes is common in obsessional disorders; endless calculation of usefulness characterises narcissism; and so on.

The delineation of B cognition is based on studies undertaken in the 1950s. Like William James before him, Maslow was interested in his subjects' spontaneous experiences of transcendence, particularly those taking the form of episodic 'peak' experiences. These experiences can occur in many circumstances: through intense experiences of love or moments of creative productivity, or when the mind is simply in a particularly relaxed and idling state. They have a number of psychological characteristics, which Maslow has listed on different occasions (Maslow 1968, 1976). In probably his most comprehensive description, he distinguishes the following qualities (Maslow 1968: 74–96):

1 perception of the object as a self-sufficient whole
2 percepts exclusively and fully attended to
3 perception freed from human motivations

4   perceptions richer in quality
5   perceptions impersonal
6   perceptions self-justifying, having intrinsic value
7   characteristic disorientation in time and space
8   perceptions experienced only as good and desirable
9   perceptions represent absolute, independent reality
10 a passive and receptive quality of 'choiceless awareness'
11 feelings of wonder, awe, reverence and humility
12 a sense of unity between all that is perceived
13 ability to perceive the concrete and the abstract at the same time
14 dichotomies, polarities and conflicts resolved or transcended
15 experiences of love, compassion or of acceptance from a 'godlike' standpoint
16 perception idiographic and classification of it resisted
17 the loss of negative feelings of fear, anxiety, inhibition, defensiveness, and control
18 a dynamic parallelism between inner and outer, with the person coming closer to his or her own being.

Reports such as those cited in Chapter 2 suggest that it is unlikely that mindful awareness as experienced by anyone who has undergone significant training will tally with fewer than half the qualities on this list. But it is also unlikely that it will match with all of them, many corresponding instead to a level that Cloninger had seen as transcending mindfulness in referring to a higher level in terms of spontaneous contemplation. Despite the synthesising power of Cloninger's work and its placing 'mindfulness' within a spectrum of health, it is the detail of Maslow's descriptions that provides the most accessible evidence of an association between perceptual transformations and positive mental health. Before investigating more specific associations between perception, mindfulness practice and mental health, we had better review the ways mental health is being used.

Mindfulness and the spectrum of health

When thinking about mental health as a positive achievement, rather than the treatment of mental illness, it seems three aspects can be distinguished. They will be referred to as able-mindedness, adaptation and autonomy. Able-mindedness reflects a capacity to withstand mental illness through immunity or avoiding its recurrence. As able-mindedness, mental health is identified with factors that serve to maintain freedom from illness and minimise the risk of mental disorders supervening.

Adaptation refers to the capacity to fit oneself to, and indeed thrive under, different circumstances. It underpins attempts to frame mental health positively in terms other than the avoidance of mental illness, such as the UK Mental Health Foundation's definition (Lee 2006).

According to it, individuals with good mental health:

- develop emotionally, creatively, intellectually and spiritually
- initiate, develop and sustain mutually satisfying personal relationships
- face problems, resolve them and learn from them
- are confident and assertive
- are aware of others and empathise with them
- use and enjoy solitude
- play and have fun
- laugh, both at themselves and at the world.

(This list certainly covers positive adjustments to others, difficulties, solitude and oneself.)

The third facet of mental health, autonomy, refers to the extent of someone's personal growth. This will involve consideration of personal adaptation, but it is essentially an expansion of the first item in the Mental Health Foundation's definition, that is, emotional, creative, intellectual and spiritual growth, valued independently of any utilitarian or functional considerations. (Self-actualisation represents one influential way of conceptualising autonomy, if not the only one.) Autonomy includes the development of 'higher' aspects of mind, whether these are experiences of transpersonal feelings, creative facility, intuition of covert aspects of reality, and so forth. While it is sometimes possible to rationalise the value of such developments in terms of their being in the interests of humanity as a whole, this is likely to be misleading. Indeed, just as they may not be guaranteed to bring an individual contentment, they may sit in considerable tension with the other two aspects of mental health. This is very literally so when highly creative people, or people open to mystical experience, also exhibit the symptoms of mental illness, and their adjustment to the demands of daily living appears to be far from satisfactory from most people's standpoint. (A useful summary of empirical work indicating that markers of positive mental health are distributed independently of symptoms of frank mental illness has been provided by Corey Keyes. However, Keyes' (2003) own equation of positive mental health with what he terms emotional, psychological and social well-being falls entirely within the scope of 'adaptation' as it is used here.)

Out of these three aspects, able-mindedness may yet prove to be the most significant in relation to mindfulness. Depression is expected to become second only to heart disease on the World Health Organisation's table of disease impact. Preventative measures are urgently needed. However, while mindfulness may appear to be readily learned, the findings of outcome studies, as well as the literature on its side effects, suggest at present that its prophylactic value is restricted to a subpopulation of people prone to depression (cf. Chapter 4, p. 91).

How might mindfulness enhance health with respect to adaptation and autonomy? We have already reviewed significant evidence that involvement in meditative pursuits does not necessarily guarantee health in either sense (cf. Chapters 2 and 4). From his clinical experience, John Suler identified the following ten negative motivations (or 'psychodynamic issues') for people to pursue meditation; when they are active, the student is likely to face defensive stasis, rather than greater self-awareness and transformation:

1   fear of autonomy
2   refusal to assume responsibility
3   withdrawal from relationships (as a rationalisation of fears of intimacy and closeness)
4   substitution for grief and mourning
5   avoidance of anxiety-arousing emotions (e.g. aggression)
6   passivity and dependence (as avoidance of competition)
7   self-punitive guilt (assuaged through ascetic routines)
8   competitiveness and the quest for perfection (expressed as spiritual pride)
9   devaluation of reason and intellect (with avoidance of self-reflection)
10 escape from other kinds of intrapsychic experience (e.g. denied aspects of self).

(Suler 1993: 142–6)

Suler's observations not only summarise points of practical importance, but also highlight the normative values of a traditional psychotherapeutic approach. From this perspective, mental health is identified with a flexible, empathic, emotionally available self that can take and assert responsibility, alongside growing capacities for feeling, intimacy, thinking and tolerance of reality. There is an unashamed model of self-development here that is apparently in conflict with meditative pursuits because these might subvert the very development the therapist is seeking. There has been a rich tradition of suspicion of this kind within the psychoanalytic tradition. It gave rise to Freud's own conceptualisation of the 'nirvana principle' in the service of the death instinct (Freud 1924), as well as the following trenchant judgement by him on the uselessness of Jungian therapies that appeared to him to ignore basic psychological realities:

> How the New Zürich therapy has shaped itself under such tendencies I can convey by means of reports of a patient who was himself obliged to experience it. 'Not the slightest effort was made to consider the past or the transferences. Whenever I thought that the latter were touched, they were explained as a mere symbol of the libido. The moral instructions were very beautiful and I followed them faithfully, but I did not advance one step. This was more distressing to me than to the physician, but how could I help it? – Instead of freeing me analytically, each session made new and tremendous demands on me, on the fulfilment of which the overcoming of the neurosis was supposed to depend. Some of these demands were: inner concentration by means of introversion, religious meditation, living together with my wife in loving devotion, etc. It was almost beyond my power, since it really amounted to a radical transformation of the whole spiritual man. I left the analysis as a poor sinner with the strongest feelings of contrition and the very best resolutions, but at the same time with the deepest discouragement. All that this physician recommended any pastor would have advised, but where was I to get the strength?'
> (Freud 1914a: 63–4)

The most incisive analytic critique of how and why meditative training may fail to help people overcome basic and long-standing difficulties with adaptation is that it underestimates our natural gift for self-deception, because there is insufficient understanding of unconscious mental processes. This is the view of Barry Magid, a psychoanalyst and Zen teacher, whose opinions reflect many years spent providing clinical services to experienced meditators (Magid 2002). Magid's experience also underlines how decisive the contribution of the meditation teacher can be in determining whether meditation serves either to perpetuate long-standing psychological difficulties, or to support independent psychotherapeutic efforts to resolve them.

There are, of course, considerable paradoxes in claims about the non-therapeutic potential of meditation. Chapter 4 reported some expectations that mindfulness practice would be clinically useful in the very areas of intimate relationships and self-functioning that are apparently being denied or bypassed here. It might be claimed that these criticisms are more likely to apply to the limitations of more concentrative forms of meditative practice. Mindfulness could be relatively immune if, performed properly, it would always facilitate experiencing inner events (however unpleasant) closely, objectively and acceptingly, as an alternative to defensive avoidance.

Engler on the fruits of mindfulness

Such claims and counterclaims can only be decided by experience. Someone well placed to do so is Jack Engler, who has many years' personal experience as a psychotherapist and a teacher of insight meditation. Engler had been a principal investigator in the study of perception among Western and Eastern mindfulness meditators summarised in Chapter 2. The apparently much slower progress and lower achievement of the Western meditators this revealed indicated to him that the Westerners' internal emotional and psychological difficulties interfered with their capacity to be mindful. He felt Eastern subjects, relatively lacking in such conflicts, progressed much further, more rapidly. Engler found support for these inferences by reverting to traditional clinical methods for interpreting the subjects' responses to the Rorschach projective test in his secondary analysis of the study's findings (Brown and Engler 1986).

As a psychotherapist, Engler had taken care to ensure that the engagement of affect as well as cognition was not ignored when explaining the traditional Buddhist understanding of the conditioning of perception to Western students. Together with his own experiences of the co-occurrence of psychological and meditational difficulties in patients and students, Engler came to an important, developmental formulation of the relative contributions of psycho-therapy and meditation to health:

> Problems in love and work, and issues around trust and intimacy in relationships in particular, can't be resolved simply by watching the moment-to-moment flow of thoughts, feelings, and sensations in the mind. Thirty years of watching students try this approach bear that out.
>
> (Engler 2003: 45)

Twenty years earlier, Engler had distinguished three distinct types of psychopathology (Engler 1986). These represent a develop-mental sequence, and can be characterised in terms of different types of ego functioning. He observed that there is no real equi-valence between the first two of these and anything in Buddhist psychology, because of the latter's lack of interest in psychological development. However, both of them will be familiar to most Western psychotherapists. The first type of organisation, attributed to early failures in the differentiation between self and others and in the establishment of a cohesive sense of self, is associated clinically with the features of borderline psychopathology. Loss of continuity in the sense of self, extreme affects, highly distorted experiences of others (which may be linked to extreme and inap-propriate reactions to them), and even hallucinatory phenomena are typical.

The second type of organisation is one in which a relatively differentiated and integrated sense of self is present, alongside actively warded-off feelings and impulses. This is associated clinically with neurotic psychopathology in which high levels of anxiety are experienced. The patient's range of feeling, perception and action is restricted as part of an adaptation to the relatively stable exclusion of some contents from consciousness. Only in the third type of organisation is the self well-differentiated and integ-rated and free to function relatively effectively.

Engler sees distinct implications for meditation and therapy with regard to the first of these states. Essentially, mindfulness practice has no part to play in its alleviation, because the uncovering action of mindfulness is likely to amplify the diffusion of identity that pre-exists in this kind of personality organisation. The attendant risk is that the very fragile, residual self-structure present would be over-whelmed by the contradictory and intense affects and impulses that would be uncovered. Engler points out that this is particularly important to recognise, because people suffering from such states of mind are quite likely to turn to meditation in an effort to find the calm and detachment they lack. He notes that, if they begin intensive mindfulness practice, their increasing disorientation and distress will take expression in extreme reactions to the meditation teacher – a situation with which teachers are all too familiar. Engler feels that, if meditation has a role here, it is likely to be in the form of concentrative practices that help to focus attention elsewhere and can lead to positive feelings of well-being.

He says very little about the second state, despite the fact that much of the material already reviewed in Chapters 3 and 4 illustrates how the judicious use of mindfulness might, through reassimilation of fended-off contents, lead to the kind of internal mental reorganisation that would restore a well-differentiated and integrated self. However, the omission may be significant in the light of his own (and Suler's) observations on the relative impotence of meditation in resolving difficulties in the areas of trust, intimacy and, by implication, conflicts concerning sexual wishes. While these can have underlying psychological patterns that resemble those found in, say, some conflicts surrounding the expression of aggression and assertion, I have yet to meet an experienced clinician who felt the most intimate relational problems could be resolved in the absence of a close working relationship with a therapist (or thera-peutic group) or without experience of actual relationships outside therapy. However, the question of whether there may be any intrinsic therapeutic limits to mindfulness here is complicated by the context of intensive mindfulness practice that Engler is referring to – that is, a quasi-religious setting. Different attitudes concerning intimacy and sexuality may be being explicitly or implicitly con-veyed there that complicate attempts to confront this kind of difficulty through mindful uncovering, in a way that may not apply to other kinds of personal difficulty.

In passing over this whole topic of mindfulness' possible role with problems arising from his second kind of self, Engler con-tinues to side rather fatalistically with the outlook of traditional teachers. He links Western students' poor progress to their pre-occupations with internal contents. A quotation he offers elsewhere from a visiting Asian teacher seems apposite: 'Many Western students do not meditate. They do therapy. They do not go deep with mindfulness' (Engler 1986: 29).

In fact, it seems Engler's principal purpose in delineating the three developmentally distinct states is to highlight the peculiarities of the third and most developed state. And these are absolutely central to the concerns of this chapter. In the West, the third state, in which the self is simultaneously well differentiated, integrated and apparently stable, is regarded as normal; in fact, healthy. According to Engler, it represents a distinct form of pathology, albeit a kind of pathology that is not recognised in the West. The issue is one of 'conditioned states', in which the very achievement of a stable sense of self and of the relations it has with objects beyond it constitutes a problem. Rephrased in psychotherapeutic language, this self remains a form of arrested development through unnecessary fixation. Engler sees mindfulness meditation as the therapy within Buddhism whose objective is to alleviate the suffering that follows from living with a self of this kind. The effects of mindfulness that were explained in Chapter 1 in terms of the categories of Buddhist psychology can, in psychotherapeutic terms, be said to 'set ego and object relations development in motion again from a point of relative arrest' (Engler 1986: 48). Engler is making a direct comparison here with the uncovering action of psychoanalysis, while conceding that, in so far as the two practices achieve this internal freeing, they do so by very different means. According to him, mindfulness works by watching the reversal of the representational processes that give rise to the sense of 'self' and 'object' so that these are deconstructed into their elementary components, with a fundamental reversal of the way the world appears.

In his more recent comments, Engler (2003) admits limitations to his developmental perspective. The idea that an unconditioned state might be deliberately attained from conditioned ones is particularly problematic, as it is inherently contradictory (cf. Krishnamurti's comments on this point, p. 124 above). Because of its utter difference from apparently static selves, Engler joins Coltart and others in suggesting that the deconstructed self that is liberated (and which corresponds to the concepts of 'no self'; 'not I'; 'no mind'; 'big mind', and so on, favoured by other writers) does not have to replace the ordinarily healthy one. What matters is that an utterly free process is no longer impeded. As this becomes paramount, the criteria for health and suffering can also shift. Engler describes how, with increasing experience of mindfulness, ordinary operations of registering pleasure or constancy become sources of pain

> in this state of awareness. Any approach/avoidance response to pleasure and pain, no matter how 'normal' in everyday experience – the simplest responses of attraction and aversion, wanting and not wanting, preferring pleasure and avoiding pain, wanting this and not wanting that – irrespective of their particular aims and objects – is experienced as an extraordinarily painful and misguided effort to block the natural flow of events. Any attempt to constellate a separate and continuous representation of self, or to preferentially identify with some self-representations as 'me' and extrude others as 'not-me' is experienced as an equally futile and painful attempt to interrupt, undo, or alter self-representations as a flow of moment-to-moment constructions.
>
> (Engler 2003: 69–70)

By now, there is little question of the no-self state being healthy because of some function it has. It is preferred because it is a fuller expression of our nature, a state that can be identified with being itself. There is a sense here in which such contentions cannot be a matter of argument. Only experience can convince. However, as Stephen Mitchell demonstrates in a response to Engler's paper, it is possible to retain scepticism of such claims, while remaining sympathetic to a positive, transpersonal conception of health (Mitchell 2003).

Being, being mindful and being healthy

Our earlier discussion of well-being had taken us to the beguiling threshold of Maslow's being world. The transformations in his self-actualised subjects' sense of themselves and of the rest of reality, and their abilities to interact easily and even inspire those around them, were related to a perceptual change expressed as their openness to peak experiences. Maslow describes these peak experiences as introducing a fusion of experience and value, so that self-actualised people have a very clear sense of what is intrinsically good in the moral sense. 'Peak experiences' have an astonishing fluidity and vitality that fit well with Engler's observations on the perception of everything being in motion. However, they do not seem to carry the painful sensitivity Engler reports in relation to any perceived obstruction to an ideal state of absolute flow.

Can anything meaningful be made of this contrast? One thing both sets of reported experience are touching on are ideals and values. It seems likely that heightened perception challenges ordinary conceptions of the fact/value divide. This is not to say that Maslow's account, for instance, is accurate in all circumstances. The premonitions it appears to offer of a world of absolute values informing events appears to be a very comforting one. It coheres beautifully with his own hierarchical analysis of human motivation and needs. Indeed, it has been an extraordinary twentieth-century reworking of Plato's ontology in contemporary terms. However, some awkward questions persist. How far had Maslow's psychology been shaped in response to his own needs, rather than being a necessary interpretation of the observations available to him? In a review of this work, his own student, Richard Lowry, comments that Maslow's work on peak experiences and self-actualisation never gained the professional acceptance that his work on the hierarchy of motivation had. Lowry outlines how Maslow came to acknowledge for himself that his selection of candidates for his self-actualisation studies reflected a wish to understand the lives of people that he personally idealised (Lowry 1999). This, rather than extraneous psychological considerations, seemed to determine the template according to which his candidates were measured. The admirable characteristics of the self-actualised person were themselves an 'ideal type' (in the Weberian sense) that no single individual ever matched in their entirety. What is more, the idea that Maslow proceeded from an idea of health to discover that what healthy people have in common is B values was illusory. As Lowry notes, Maslow admits in his own journal that he was, in fact, selecting people for study because they used 'B language' and excluding others if they did not, even if they still met the health criteria for inclusion. What was presented as being resulted from bias.

Nevertheless, Maslow's increasing preoccupation with value as something that is embedded may reflect an empirical truth of a different kind. It can seem that the uncovering attention of mindfulness works to reveal values that lend experience a form of coherence that is not ordinarily apparent. It is not uncommon for this to find expression as meditators believe they are discovering some kind of transmissible truth or wisdom about reality as their explorations proceed. This may be further encouraged if an expectation that it will result in 'insight' is widely accepted, although teachers in the mindfulness/vipassana tradition tend to emphasise the immediate, intuitive and non-conceptual nature of realisations concerning the ultimate nature of things and to be dismissive of students' verbal formulations. In Engler's description of perceptual insight, there was a striking vision of how things should be, the sensations of pain he reports cohering with this.

A sense of intrinsic value is evident there too. But is it finally a necessary one, reflecting an absolute quality of being? Or is it a contingent one that would be resolved through further refinement of the meditator's perception? This question goes to the heart of the traditional conception of mindfulness and its role in personal transformation that was outlined in Chapter 1. There we saw how the final section of the greater *sutta* on the foundations of mindfulness dealt with mindfulness of the mind's contents in terms of teaching or *dhamma*. These teachings comprise statements about the basic divisions of reality (physical and psychological) that, as their labels' language of 'hindrances' or 'enlightenment factors' suggests, are inseparable from values. Yet, the *sutta* is curiously ambiguous concerning the approach the meditator might adopt in relation to these elements. The account provided in Chapter 1 reflects prevalent teaching that a kind of submission to the eternal truth of this *dhamma* is required (cf. p. 17). Perception is to be aligned with it, all experience being appreciated as conforming with its categories. (The responses of the Eastern master to Engler and Brown's projective testing in Chapter 2 seems an excellent example of this.) This would affirm a transcendent sense of order that supports many noble and subtle values, including those concerning health, that called the satisfactoriness of the ordinary self so sharply into question.

However, another reading of the treatment of mental objects in the *sutta* is possible. It is the simplest, in that mental objects, even *dhamma* teachings, are treated no differently from anything else that presents to awareness. The task is to penetrate deeply into their arising and passing away too. They are no more welcome to take root than any other object or mental content, however great the temptation. As a repository for values central to the whole system of Buddhist thought, mind objects such as the Four Noble Truths would be the most tenacious, still conditioning a monk's perception once all else has been allowed to fall away. On this alternative reading of the *sutta*, they become the final obstacle rather than the final truth. Once they, too, can be experienced like any other object, mindfulness has been truly established. Only then does a process without any restriction or conditioning remain.

Words are likely to be of very limited help in portraying such a state. By extrapolating from mindfulness' apparently distinguishable psychological actions of dechaining, resensing and decentering (cf. Chapter 4), something of the experience of things once awareness is freer might be inferred. All three actions would now be unfettered, bringing about a reversal of perception. Each component, however small, would have a quality of completeness in itself. They would also be vividly alive, interpenetrating and containing their opposite. And, instead of an observer reaching out to the world with awareness, there would only be an impersonal awareness in which everything was held. There is a logic to this, and a resonance with several (if not all) of Maslow's observations on peak experience and B perception. If such a shift in perception also brings with it a fundamentally different relationship to reality, which is precisely what talking about 'being' here implies, then former judgements about what is healthy and what is not lose their relevance. What represents either adjustment or autonomy in relation to the ground of our being may have little in common with what counts as adjustment or autonomy in the context of the familiar, conditioned world. Indeed, it is hard to imagine, if terms such as adjustment and autonomy retain any meaning in this different context, how they would not be the same thing.

If mindfulness actually led its practitioners completely out of themselves, bringing them directly into a non-dual universe permeated by B values, there would arguably be little more to say on the question of health. Old standards need not apply. However, despite traditional teaching's implication that mindfulness provides sufficient means, this is not necessarily the case. Cloninger, for instance, had not linked mindfulness to a world of this kind (which corresponds to his contemplative level) but to one that is transitional between ordinary modes of awareness and others associated with even greater inner freedom. The retention of an attenuated sense of oneself, attuned to different aspects of sensory experience but in which one still relates to it as an observer, was confirmed by the group interview with experienced mindfulness teachers reported in Chapter 2.

John Welwood is another clinician who has not been afraid to consider the ontological implications of his far-ranging experiences in psychotherapeutic work. His 'transpersonal' outlook is indebted to Buddhist schools that came after the Theravadan traditions from which the basic theory of mindfulness has been drawn. However, Welwood (2000) recognises a very similar spectrum for the organisation of awareness to Cloninger. Mindfulness comes about midway along Welwood's sequence also. What is singular to his approach is the description of a distinctive cognitive process for each stage. In sequence, these are as follows:

1   *Conceptual reflection.* A sense of separation and flexibility is achieved through articulation of experience.
2   *Phenomenological reflection.* There is an openness to direct and preconceptual experience, untrammelled by language.
3   *Reflective witnessing.* Here, 'bare, mindful attention' attends to the flow of experience rather than to individual objects within it.
4   *Transmutation.* A qualitative shift permits immediate awareness of life and intelligence within coarser perceptions.
5   *Continuing self-liberation.* With the disappearance of a sense of an observing self, one of unitary presence supervenes.

Its midway position in schemes like Welwood's and Cloninger's indicates that mindfulness is a transformative process, assisting access to more refined modes of being conscious. However, its role in the kinds of personal development being considered here appears to be a transitional, rather than an ultimately liberating, one. This status seems congruent with mindfulness' ambiguous contemporary image as a health-promoting as well as a spiritual practice. In fostering qualities of equanimity and tranquillity alongside an unusually acute and open awareness, it is likely to be adaptive in many contexts where resilience and performance are favoured. Mindfulness resembles Csikszentmihalyi's 'flow' in this, if differing a little in the quality of awareness that results (and differing from flow a lot in the limitlessness of the situations to which, by definition, it can be opened). This developmentally transitional quality of mindfulness indicates a potential to promote a form of personal growth that, like other versions of autonomy, cannot be reduced entirely to either able-mindedness or adaptation, although it subsumes them. At the same time, this potential is not identical to kindred developments such as 'self-actualisation'. To understand just what its contribution to personal autonomy may be, and the ways in which it may remain limited, we are likely to have to fall back on two pillars of this book, Buddhist theory and science.

Buddhist theory is quite clear that a truly stable equilibrium is attained only once a fundamental quality of no-self (*anatta*) is realised, dissolving distinctions between individual beings. Psychologically, too, this seems an unequivocal basis on which distinctions between able-mindedness, adaptation and autonomy not only recede, but vanish altogether. However, we have seen in Chapters 1 and 5 some ways in which there is a possibly necessary ambiguity in Buddhism concerning the extent to which mindfulness, as one component of a system whose interrelations can seem infinitely intricate, represents sufficient means for realising such a state. (Examples were the need for the action of mindfulness to be complemented by 'clear comprehension' (cf. p. 19 above) or practices in which exercises to develop mindfulness are supplemented by others that foster appreciation of more subtle, transpersonal feelings (cf. p. 20). Others could be cited.)

As for science, the evidence from qualitative and physiological studies of mindfulness meditators in Chapter 2 appears to mirror this ambiguity. Considered against findings from people accessing states where *anatta* is more evident, these support the notion that, irrespective of their transformational potential, mindful states of consciousness occupy the middle ground within a broader spectrum. Moreover, observations made in Chapters 2 and 4 concerning the coincidence of mindful practices and psychiatric symptoms (as well as work cited in the previous section of this chapter) indicate how, despite occasionally wilful attempts to show otherwise, science does not recognise neat lines between psychological states taken as indicative of positive mental health and other experiences usually attributed to mental illness.

Part of the genius of Buddhism has been to link aspects of spiritual attainment with psychological changes that can be expressed in cognitive terms. This has made it appealing to people in the West who are respectful of reason, and who believe in human potential, but distrust deist religions. However, it appears that the more ultimate goals heave into view, the clearer the gulf between Buddhism's values and those of Western psychology becomes – however 'positive' the latter may take itself to be. It would seem that, so far as mindfulness is concerned, thinking of health in terms of positive states or qualities of being is not necessarily helpful. Despite doing so, we have still not identified what is most distinctive to mindfulness' contribution.

Health, self-knowledge and suffering

There seem to be several ways to go at this point. One is to get increasingly preoccupied with goals (and there are few more compelling than health) and their interrelationship with mindfulness and the practices that foster it. The project that Shapiro *et al.* (2006) have initiated into the colouring of practice by values, alongside other apparently determinant factors, is an important response to this kind of dilemma. We saw in Chapter 2 how these inter-relationships, which cast doubt on the apparent unity of mindfulness, deserve and are amenable to further empirical exploration.

Another response is to question the value of explorations of the goal of health in the kind of terms adopted above, in favour of recollection of some aspects of the West's indigenous transformative psychologies. As we noted in Chapter 3, interest in mindfulness is being accompanied by a wider resurgence in the popularity of Buddhistic ideas. Among the consequences of this are a growing acceptance in the West of generalised references to Buddhist teachings, such as the self being illusory or everyone being responsible for their own salvation. Alongside this, and despite its actual consequences for others, the more uncomfortable particulars of self-delusion can go unexamined. Whether or not such blindness misrepresents Buddhism, it represents a failure to appreciate or recollect lessons available through Western depth psychologies. A loss of working familiarity with the understandings that have informed psychoanalysis and analytic psychology – for instance, how it is no more possible to escape our psychological shadow (comprising all that we disown) than our physical one – means people are more likely to be blind to themselves. It also suggests they will be condemned to rediscover them in some other way.

One frequent and widely shared aspect of self-delusion is an almost insatiable need to idealise – whether through fantasies about attaining states of radiant enlightenment, or in dreams of treatments that will magic away every trouble and worry. The phenomenon of mindfulness, like the chimera of health, is open to idealisation in both of these ways. Paradoxically, being driven by ideals (rather than resting in moment-to-moment awareness) seems like a recipe for disabling mindfulness, because more and more ground for dissent opens up. This is not inevitable. Mindfulness teachers such as Jon Kabat-Zinn do recognise that 'We need to develop and refine our mind and its capacities for seeing and knowing, for recognizing and transcending whatever motives and concepts and habits of unawareness may have generated or compounded the difficulties we find ourselves embroiled within' (Kabat-Zinn 2005: 62). But what is the nature of that need?

A third response to the impasse over health is to seek an alternative basis for understanding and practice that still bridges Buddhist and Western outlooks. A prime candidate would be the apparent antithesis of health: suffering. Perhaps suffering is where this exploration needs to finish. In Chapter 1, we saw that the most fundamental assumption within Buddhist ontology is that reality has three inescapable characteristics – those of suffering (*dukkha*), impermanence (*anicca*) and no-self (*anatta*). The pursuit of health has led us progressively toward the uplands of *anatta* and away from the other bases, including suffering. This pursuit has also threatened to go beyond mindfulness, as well as providing more and more reminders of the residual differences, if not incompatibilities, between Buddhist and Western approaches. If, instead, we ask what common concern motivates the two traditions – Buddhism as a practical discipline, and the Western tradition of practical philosophy that modern psychotherapy has descended from (Mace 1999a) – we return to suffering. Working with mindfulness enhances sensitivity to the presence and the nature of suffering. The importance of responding to suffering is the essential common ground between Buddhist and Western practices, as mindfulness becomes an aid to health.

In Buddhist theory, the roots of suffering lie in desire, aversion and delusion. It could be argued that recognition of the clinical importance of each of these, to the relative exclusion of the others, has inspired the psychoanalytic, behavioural and cognitive movements, respectively, within modern psychotherapy. From the Buddhist perspective, desire, aversion and delusion are interdependent, with the implication that therapeutic approaches that embody mindfulness fully would have the capacity to work with all three. At present, we have noted that existing mindfulness-based therapies appear to differ in their actions. These differences can be analysed in terms of the combination of dechaining, resensing and decentering that seems characteristic of a given approach. Analysis of these constituent actions was founded in experience as well as inference, being supported by introspection as well as external observation of clinical effects and hypothesis testing. However provisional this three-action model may prove, there are also striking complementaries between dechaining and desire; resensing and aversion; and decentering and delusion, where one is an antidote to the other. While mindfulness-based treatment approaches have developed in significant ways, their evident differences and limitations suggest that, like more traditional psychotherapies, they may not have realised their full potential to influence mental suffering. If they are to do so, their prospects seem likely to depend upon fuller appreciation of the interconnections between insights from therapy, theory and science.

Conclusions

Mental health can be understood as freedom from mental disorder (able-mindedness), as optimal adaptation, or as fulfilment of potential (autonomy). Developments in physiology as well as psychology have made it possible to sketch a model of well-being that interconnects all three conceptions of positive mental health and links them to different forms of awareness. The phenomenon of 'flow' provides a good instance of how a healthy state can be identified with its attentional characteristics, although its range is limited. When mindfulness is considered in relation to positive mental health, different aspects of its action come to the fore than in discussions of its strictly therapeutic use. Its role in preventing emotional disorder is likely to be important in relation to able-mindedness. Its potential contribution to adaptation is less clear at present, with limits apparent in how far it could contribute to healing relationships, for instance.

Consideration of health as self-development highlights the difference between an individualistic psychology and one where the ordinary self is, by definition, less than healthy. Mindfulness may offer an accessible way of loosening (but not eliminating) this self-structure, although pre-existing psychological difficulties are likely to complicate the process. Developments of this kind are probably less dependent on being healthy and on being well adapted than Maslow's being psychology had suggested. Identifying health with more traditional spiritual ideals opens up many incompatibilities between Buddhist and Western approaches to well-being. These contradictions are less apparent when mindfulness is simply a means of being directly aware of suffering, a conclusion that fits well with the uses it has found to date.

Appendix: Mindfulness centres

The following centres organise courses and training programmes and support research into the application of mindfulness.

Center for Mindfulness in Medicine, Health Care, and Society
55 Lake Avenue North
Worcester, MA 01655
USA
Tel: (01) 508-856-2656
Email: mindfulness@umassmed.edu
Website: www.umassmed.edu/cfm

Centre for Mindfulness Research and Practice
Institute of Medical and Social Care Research
University of Wales, Bangor
Dean Street Building
Bangor LL57 1UT
UK
Tel: (44) 1248 382939
Fax: (44) 1248 383982
Email: mindfulness@bangor.ac.uk.
Website: www.bangor.ac.uk/mindfulness

A number of organisations providing training in specific formal techniques of mindfulness meditation can be located by searching the World Wide Web for 'insight' or 'vipassana' meditation schools.

References

Albeniz, A. and Holmes, J. (2000) Meditation: concepts, effects and uses in therapy. *International Journal of Psychotherapy*, **5**, 49–58.

APA (2004) *Diagnostic and Statistical Manual of Mental Disorders IVth edn (Text Revision)*. Washington, DC: American Psychiatric Association.

Astley, N. (ed.) (2002) *Staying Alive*. Tarset: Bloodaxe.

Austin, J. H. (1998) *Zen and the Brain*. Cambridge MA: MIT Press.

Bach, P. and Hayes, S. H. (2002) The use of acceptance and commitment therapy to prevent the rehospitalisation of psychotic patients: a randomized controlled trial. *Journal of Consulting and Clinical Psychology*, **70**, 1129–39.

Bach, P., Gaudiano, B., Pankey, J. *et al.* (2006) Acceptance, mindfulness, values, and psychosis: applying ACT to the chronically mentally ill. In *Mindfulness-Based Treatment Approaches. Clinician's Guide to Evidence Base and Applications* (ed. R. Baer), New York: Academic Press, pp. 94–116.

Baer, R. (2006) Meditation, mindfulness, and psychological functioning in a sample of experienced meditators. In *4th Annual International Conference on Mindfulness in Medicine, Health Care and Society*. Worcester, MA.

Baer, R. A. (2003) Mindfulness training as a clinical intervention: a conceptual and empirical review. *Clinical Psychology: Science and Practice*, **19**, 125–43.

Baer, R. A., Smith, G. and Allen, K. (2004) Assessment of mindfulness by self-report: the Kentucky Inventory of Mindfulness Skills. *Assessment*, **11**, 191–206.

Becker, D. and Shapiro, D. (1981) Physiological responses to clicks during Zen, yoga and TM meditation. *Psychophysiology*, **18**, 694–9.

Bion, W. (1970) *Attention and Interpretation*. London: Tavistock.

Bishop, S. (2002) What do we really know about mindfulness-based stress reduction? *Psychosomatic Medicine*, **64**, 71–84.

Bishop, S., Lau, M., Segal, Z. *et al.* (2003) Development and validation of the Toronto Mindfulness Scale. In *International Meeting of the Society for Psychotherapy Research*. Weimar.

Bishop, S., Lau, M., Shapiro, S. *et al.* (2004) Mindfulness: a proposed operational definition. *Clinical Psychology: Science and Practice*, **11**, 230–41.

Bloch, A., Shear, M., Markowitz, J. *et al.* (1993) An empirical study of defense mechanisms in dysthymia. *American Journal of Psychiatry*, **150**, 1194–8.

Bohdi, B. T. (2000) *Connected Discourses of the Buddha*. Boston, MA: Wisdom Publications.

Brazier, C. (2003) *Buddhist Psychology*. London: Robinson.

Brown, D. and Engler, J. (1986) The stages of mindfulness meditation: a validation study. In *Transformations of Consciousness* (Also in *Journal of Transpersonal Psychology* (1980), **12**, 143–92) (eds K. Wilber, J. Engler and D. Brown). Boston, MA: Shambhala, pp. 161–91.

Brown, K. and Ryan, R. (2003) The benefits of being present: mindfulness and its role in psychological well-being. *Journal of Personality and Social Psychology*, **84**, 822–48.

—— (2004) Perils and promise in defining and measuring mindfulness: observations from experience. *Clinical Psychology: Science and Practice*, **11**, 242–8.

Buchheld, N., Grossman, P. and Walach, H. (2002) Measuring mindfulness in insight meditation (vipassana) and meditation-based psychotherapy: the development of the Freiburg Mindfulness Inventory (FMI). *Journal of Meditation and Meditation Research*, **1**, 11–34.

Buddhaghosa, B. (1999) *Vissudhimagga or the Path of Purification* (trans. N. Thera). Seattle, WA: BPS Pariyatti Editions.

Carson, J., Carson, K., Gil, K. *et al.* (2004) Mindfulness-based relationship enhancement. *Behavior Therapy*, **35**, 471–94.

—— (2006) Mindfulness-based relationship enhancement in couples. In *Mindfulness-Based Treatment Approaches: Clinician's Guide to Evidence Base and Applications* (ed. R. Baer), Burlington, MA: Academic Press, pp. 309–31.

Chadwick, P., Newman Taylor, K. and Abba, N. (2005) Mindfulness groups for people with psychosis. *Behavioural and Cognitive Psychotherapy*, **33**, 351–9.

Charmaz, K. (2001) Grounded theory: methodology and theory construction. In *International Encyclopedia of the Social and Behavioural Sciences* (eds N. Smeser and P. Baltes), Amsterdam: Pergamon, pp. 6396–9.

Cloninger, C. (2004) *Feeling Good: The Science of Well-Being*. New York: Oxford University Press.

Cloninger, C. R. (1999) A new conceptual paradigm from genetics and psychobiology for the science of mental health. *Australian and New Zealand Journal of Psychiatry*, **33**, 174–86.

Cloninger, C. R., Bayon, C. and Svrakic, D. M. (1998) Measurement of temperament and character in mood disorders: a model of fundamental states as personality types. *Journal of Affective Disorders*, **51**, 21–32.

Coltart, N. (1992) Attention. In *Slouching Towards Bethlehem* (ed. N. Coltart), London: Free Association Books, pp. 176–93.

—— (1998) Slouching towards Buddhism: in conversation with Anthony Molino. In *The Couch and the Tree* (ed. A. Molino), New York: North Point Press, pp. 170–82.

Csikszentmihalyi, M. (1990) *Flow: The Psychology of Optimal Experience*. New York: Harper & Row.

Davidson, R., Kabat-Zinn, J., Schumacher, J. *et al.* (2003) Alterations in brain and immune function produced by mindfulness meditation. *Psychosomatic Medicine*, **65**, 564–70.

Dilbeck, M. and Bronson, E. (1981) Short-term longitudinal effects of the transcendental meditation technique on EEG power and coherence. *International Journal of Neuroscience*, **14**, 147–51.

Dubois, R. (1966) *Man and His Environment: Biomedical Knowledge and Social Action*. Washington, DC: World Health Organization.

Dunn, B., Hartigan, J. and Mikulas, W. (1999) Concentration and mindfulness meditations: unique forms of consciousness? *Applied Psychophysiology and Biofeedback*, **24**, 147–65.

Engler, J. (1986) Therapeutic aims in psychotherapy and meditation: developmental stages in the representation of the self. In *Transformations of Consciousness* (originally in *Journal of Transpersonal Psychology* (1984), **16**, 25–61) (eds K. Wilber, J. Engler and D. Brown), Boston, MA: Shambhala, pp. 17–51.

—— (2003) Being somebody and being nobody. In *Psychoanalysis and Buddhism* (ed. J. Safran), Boston, MA: Wisdom Publications, pp. 35–100.

Epstein, M. (1984) On the neglect of evenly suspended attention. *Journal of Transpersonal Psychology*, **16**, 193–205.

—— (1996) *Thoughts Without a Thinker*. London: Duckworth.

—— (1999) *Going to Pieces without Falling Apart*. London: Thorsons.

Fava, G. (2000) Subclinical symptoms in mood disorders: pathophysiological and therapeutic implications. *Psychological Medicine*, **29**, 47–61.

Fennell, M. (2004) Depression, low self-esteem and mindfulness. *Behavior Research and Therapy*, **42**, 1053–67.

Fonagy, P., Gergely, G., Jurist, E. *et al.* (2002) *Affect Regulation, Mentalization and the Development of the Self*. New York: Other Press.

Freud, S. (1912) Recommendations for physicians on the psycho-analytic method of treatment. In *Standard Edition*, vol. 12, London: Hogarth, pp. 109–20.

—— (1914a) *The History of the Psychoanalytic Movement*. In *Standard Edition*, vol. 14, London, Hogarth, pp. 7–66.

—— (1914b) Remembering, repeating and working through. In *Standard Edition*, vol. 12, London, Hogarth, pp. 145–56.

—— (1920) Mourning and melancholia. In *Standard Edition*, vol. 14, London, Hogarth, pp. 243–60.

—— (1923) The ego and the id. In *Standard Edition*, vol. 19, London: Hogarth, pp. 3–67.

—— (1924) The economic problem of masochism. In *Standard Edition*, vol. 19, London: Hogarth, pp. 159–72.

Gaylord, C., Orme-Johnson, D. and Travis, E. (1989) The effects of the transcendental meditation technique and progressive muscle relaxation on EEG coherence, stress reactivity and mental health in black adults. *International Journal of Neuroscience*, **46**, 77–86.

Gendlin, E. (1996) *Focusing-Oriented Psychotherapy*. New York: Guilford.

Germer, G. (2005a) Teaching mindfulness in therapy. In *Mindfulness and Psychotherapy* (eds G. Germer, R. Siegal and P. Fulton), New York: Guilford, pp. 113–29.

—— (2005b) What is mindfulness? In *Mindfulness and Psychotherapy* (eds G. Germer, R. Siegel and P. Fulton), New York: Guilford, pp. 1–27.

Germer, G., Siegel, R. and Fulton, P. (eds) (2005) *Mindfulness and Psychotherapy*. New York: Guilford.

Gethin, R. (1995) *Basics of Buddhism*. Oxford: Oxford University Press.

Gibbs, G. (2002) *Qualitative Data Analysis: Explorations with NVivo*. Buckingham: Open University Press.

Gilbert, P. (2005) *Compassion*. London: Brunner-Routledge.

Goenka, S. (1988) *Satipatthana Sutta Discourses*. Seattle, WA: Vipassana Research Publications.

Goleman, D. (1988) *The Meditative Mind*. New York: Putnam.

—— (2003) *Destructive Emotions*. New York: Bantam.

Grossman, P., Niemann, L., Schmidt, S. *et al.* (2004) Mindfulness-based stress reduction and health benefits: a meta-analysis. *Journal of Psychosomatic Research*, **57**, 35–43.

Gunaratana, H. (1992) *Mindfulness in Plain English*. Boston, MA: Wisdom Publications.

Guthrie, E. (2000) Psychotherapy for patients with complex disorders and chronic symptoms: the need for a new research paradigm. *British Journal of Psychiatry*, **177**, 131–7.

Haidt, J. (2006) *The Happiness Hypothesis*. London: Heinemann.

Hanh, T. (2002) *Anger*. Ithaca, NY: Snow Lion.

Hanh, T. N. (1991) *The Miracle of Mindfulness*. London: Rider.

Hart, W. (1988) *The Art of Living: Vipassana Meditation as Taught by S.N. Goenka*. Igatpuri: Vipassana Research Institute.

Hassed, C. (2004) Bringing holism into mainstream biomedical education. *Journal of Alternative and Complementary Medicine*, **10**, 405–7.

—— (2005a) Introducing MBSR into undergraduate medical education. In *Integrating Mindfulness-Based Interventions into Medicine, Health Care and Society*. Worcester, MA.

—— (2005b) Preliminary evaluation of the MBSR program of medical students. In *Integrating Mindfulness-Based Interventions into Medicine, Health Care and Society*. Worcester, MA.

Hayes, S., Strosahl, S. and Wilson, K. (1999) *Acceptance and Commitment Therapy*. New York: Guilford.

Helminski, K. (2000) *The Rumi Collection. An Anthology of Translations of Mevlana Jalaluddin Rumi*. Boston, MA: Shambhala.

Horney, K. (1951) The quality of the analyst's attention. In *Karen Horney: The Therapeutic Process* (ed. B. Paris), New Haven, CT: Yale University Press, pp. 186–90.

—— (1987) *Final Lectures* (ed. D. H. Ingram). New York: Norton.

Horowitz, M. (2002) Self- and relational observation. *Journal of Psychotherapy Integration*, **12**, 115–27.

James, W. (1927) *The Principles of Psychology* (3rd edn). New York: Holt.

Johnstone, L. and Dallos, R. (eds) (2006) *Formulation in Psychology and Psychotherapy*. Hove: Routledge.

Kabat-Zinn, J. (1990) *Full Catastrophe Living*. New York: Delta.

—— (1994) *Mindfulness Meditation for Everyday Life*. London: Piatkus Books.

—— (2005) *Coming to Our Senses*. New York: Hyperion.

Kabat-Zinn, J., Chapman, A. and Salmon, P. (1997) Relationship of cognitive and somatic components of anxiety to patient preference for different relaxation techniques. *Mind–Body Medicine*, **2**, 101–9.

Kabat-Zinn, J., Massion, A. and Kristeller, J. (1992) Effectiveness of a meditation-based stress reduction program in the treatment of anxiety disorders. *American Journal of Psychiatry*, **149**, 936–43.

Kant, I. (2003) *Critique of Pure Reason* (trans. N. Kemp-Smith). London: Palgrave-Macmillan.

Kasamatsu, A. and Hirai, T. (1966) An electroencephalographic study on the Zen meditation (zazen). In *Altered States of Consciousness* (3rd edn) (originally published in *Folio Psychiatrica and Neurologica Japonica* (1966), **20**, 315–36) (ed. C. Tart), San Francisco: HarperCollins, pp. 581–95.

Keyes, C. (2003) Complete mental health: an agenda for the 21st century. In *Flourishing: Positive Psychology and the Life Well-Lived* (eds C. Keyes and J. Haidt), Washington, DC: American Psychological Association, pp. 293–312.

Khantipalo, B. E. (1996) *A Treasury of Buddhist Stories from the*

Dhammapada Commentary (trans. E. R. Burlingame). Kandy: Buddhist Publication Society.

Kornfield, J. (1993) *A Path with Heart*. New York: Bantam Books.

Krishnamurti, J. (1986) *Commentaries on Living: Second Series*. London: Gollancz.

—— (1988) *Commentaries on Living: First Series* (2nd impression). London: Gollancz.

Kristeller, J. and Hallett, C. (1999) An exploratory study of a meditation-based intervention for binge eating disorder. *Journal of Health Psychology*, **4**, 357–63.

Kristeller, J., Baer, R. and Quillian-Wolever, G. (2006) Mindfulness-based approaches to eating disorders. In *Mindfulness-Based Treatment Approaches: Clinician's Guide to Evidence Base and Applications* (ed. R. Baer), Burlington, MA: Academic Press, pp. 75–91.

Kutz, I., Borysenko, J. and Benson, H. (1985a) Meditation and psycho-therapy: a rationale for the integration of dynamic psychotherapy, the relaxation response, and mindfulness meditation. *American Journal of Psychiatry*, **142**, 1–8.

Kutz, I., Leserman, J., Dorrington, C. *et al.* (1985b) Meditation as an adjunct to psychotherapy: an outcome study. *Psychotherapy and Psychosomatics*, **43**, 209–18.

Lama, D. (1997) *Healing Anger: The Power of Patience from a Buddhist Perspective*. Ithaca, NY: Snow Lion.

Lancaster, B. (2004) *Approaches to Consciousness: The Marriage of Science and Mysticism*. London: Palgrave.

Langer, S. (1989) *Mindfulness*. Cambridge, MA: Da Capo.

Lazar, S., Kerr, C., Wasserman, R. *et al.* (2005) Meditation experience is asssociated with increased cortical thickness. *Neuroreport*, **16**, 1893–7.

Leary, M. (2004) *The Curse of the Self*. New York: Oxford University Press.

Lee, M. (2006) *Promoting Mental Health and Wellbeing in Later Life*. London: Mental Health Foundation and Age Concern.

Linehan, M. M. (1993a) *Cognitive-Behavioral Treatment of Borderline Personality Disorder*. New York: Guilford.

—— (1993b) *Skills Training Manual for Treating Borderline Personality Disorder*. New York: Guilford.

Linehan, M. M., Armstrong, H. E., Suarez, A. *et al.* (1991) Cognitive-behavioral treatment of chronically parasuicidal borderline patients. *Archives of General Psychiatry*, **48**, 1060–4.

Linehan, M. M., Comtois, K. A., Murray, A. M. *et al.* (2006) Two-year randomized controlled trial and follow-up of dialectical behavior therapy vs therapy by experts for suicidal behaviors and borderline personality disorder. *Archives of General Psychiatry*, **63**, 757–66.

Lowry, R. (1999) Preface. In *Toward a Psychology of Being* (ed. R. Lowry), New York: Van Nostrand, pp. 1–20.

Lutz, A., Greischar, L., Rawlings, N. *et al.* (2004) Long-term meditators self-induce high-amplitude gamma synchrony during mental practice. *Proceedings of the National Academy of Sciences of the United States of America*, **101**, 16369–73.

Lynch, T. R., Chapman, A. L., Rosenthal, M. Z. *et al.* (2006) Mechanisms of change in dialectical behavior therapy: theoretical and empirical observations. *Journal of Clinical Psychology*, **62**, 459–80.

Ma, S. H. and Teasdale, J. D. (2004) Mindfulness-based cognitive therapy for depression: replication and exploration of differential relapse prevention effects. *Journal of Consulting and Clinical Psychology*, **72**, 31–40.

Mace, C. (ed.) (1999a) *Heart and Soul: The Therapeutic Face of Philosophy*. London: Routledge.

—— (1999b) Socratic psychotherapy. *Changes*, **17**, 161–70.

—— (2002) Groups and integration in psychotherapy. In *Integration in Psychotherapy: Theory, Models and Practice* (eds A. Bateman and J. Holmes), Oxford: Oxford University Press, pp. 69–86.

—— (2003) Psychotherapy and neuroscience: how close can they get? In *Revolutionary Connections* (eds J. Corrigal and H. Wilkinson), London: Karnac, pp. 163–74.

—— (2006) Long-term impacts of mindfulness on psychological wellbeing: new findings from qualitative research. In *Dimensions of Well-Being* (ed. A. delle Fave), Milan: FrancoAngeli, pp. 255–69.

—— (2007) Mindfulness in psychotherapy: an introduction. *Advances in Psychiatric Treatment*, **13**, 147–54.

—— (in press) Mindfulness and the technology of healing: lessons from Western practice. In *Self and No-Self* (eds D. Mathers, M. Miller and P. Anzo), Hove: Routledge.

Magid, B. (2002) *Ordinary Mind*. Boston, MA: Wisdom.

Marcus, M., Fine, P., Moeller, F. *et al.* (2003) Change in stress levels following mindfulness-based stress reduction in a therapeutic community. *Addictive Disorders*, **2**, 63–8.

Marlatt, G., Witkiewitz, K. and Dillworth, T. (2004) Vipassana meditation as a treatment for alcohol and drug use disorders. In *Mindfulness and Acceptance: Expanding the Cognitive-Behavioral Tradition* (eds S. Hayes, V. Follette and M. M. Linehan), New York: Guilford, pp. 261–87.

Martin, J. (1997) Mindfulness: a proposed common factor. *Journal of Psychotherapy Integration*, **7**, 291–312.

Mascaro, J. (1973) *The Dhammapada*. Harmondsworth: Penguin.

Maslow, A. (1954) *Personality and Motivation*. New York: Harper.

—— (1968) *Towards a Psychology of Being* (2nd edn). New York: Van Nostrand Reinhold.

—— (1976) Further notes on cognition. In *The Farther Reaches of Human Nature*, Harmondsworth: Penguin, pp. 249–55.

Mason, O. and Hargreaves, I. (2001) A qualitative study of mindfulness-based cognitive therapy for depression. *British Journal of Medical Psychology*, **74**, 197–212.

Meldman, M. (1970) *Diseases of Attention and Perception*. Oxford: Pergamon.

Miller, J., Fletcher, K. and Kabat-Zinn, J. (1995) Three-year follow-up and clinical implications of a mindfulness meditation-based stress reduction intervention in the treatment of anxiety disorders. *General Hospital Psychiatry*, **17**, 192–200.

Mitchell, S. (2003) Somebodies and nobodies. In *Psychoanalysis and Buddhism* (ed. J. Safran), Boston, MA: Wisdom, pp. 80–6.

Morgan, W. and Morgan, S. (2005) Cultivating attention and empathy. In *Mindfulness and Psychotherapy* (eds G. Germer, R. Siegal and P. Fulton), New York: Guilford, pp. 73–90.

Nakamura, J. and Csikszentmihalyi, M. (2003) The construction of meaning through vital engagement. In *Flourishing* (eds C. Keyes and J. Haidt), Washington, DC: American Psychological Association, pp. 83–104.

Nanamoli, B. (1964) *Mindfulness of Breathing (Anapanasati)* (2nd edn). Kandy: Buddhist Publication Society.

Nanamoli, B. and Bodhi, B. (1995) *The Middle Length Discourses of the Buddha (Majjhima Nikaya)*. Boston, MA: Wisdom Publications.

Neborsky, R. (2006) Brain, mind and dyadic change process. *Journal of Clinical Psychology*, **62**, 523–38.

Nolen-Hoeksema, S. and Morrow, J. (1991) A prospective-study of depression and posttraumatic stress symptoms after a natural disaster – the 1989 Loma-Prieta earthquake. *Journal of Personality and Social Psychology*, **61**, 115–21.

—— (1993) Effects of rumination and distraction on naturally-occurring depressed mood. *Cognition and Emotion*, 7, 561–70.

Nussbaum, M. (1994) *The Therapy of Desire: Theory and Practice in Hellenistic Ethics*. Princeton, NJ: Princeton University Press.

Ogden, P. and Minton, K. (2000) Sensorimotor psychotherapy: one method for processing trauma. *Traumatology*, 6(3). www.fsu.edu/~trauma/v6i3/v6i3a3.html.

Oliver, M. (1986) *Dream Work*. New York: Atlantic Monthly Press.

Pagano, R., Rose, R., Stivers, R. *et al.* (1976) Sleep during transcendental meditation. *Science*, **191**, 308–10.

Paykel, E. S., Scott, J., Teasdale, J. D. *et al.* (1999) Prevention of relapse in residual depression by cognitive therapy – a controlled trial. *Archives of General Psychiatry*, **56**, 829–35.

Peterson, C. and Seligman, M. (2004) *Character Strengths and Virtues: A*

Handbook and Classification. Washington, DC: APA/Oxford University Press.

Ramel, W., Goldin, P., Carmona, P. *et al.* (2004) The effects of mindfulness meditation on cognitive processes and affect in patients with past depression. *Cognitive Therapy and Research*, **28**, 433–55.

Reibel, D. K., Greeson, J. M., Brainard, G. C. *et al.* (2001) Mindfulness-based stress reduction and health-related quality of life in a heterogeneous patient population. *General Hospital Psychiatry*, **23**, 183–92.

Roemer, L., Salters-Pedneault, K. and Orsillo, S. (2006) Incorporating mindfulness- and acceptance-based strategies in the treatment of generalized anxiety disorder. In *Mindfulness-Based Treatment Approaches. Clinician's Guide to Evidence Base and Applications* (ed. R. Baer), Burlington, MA: Academic Press, pp. 52–74.

Rosenberg, L. (1998) *Breath by Breath: The Liberating Practice of Insight Meditation*. Boston, MA: Shambhala.

Rosenzweig, S. (2004) Integrating MBSR into a medical school curriculum. In *Integrating Mindfulness-Based Interventions into Medicine, Health Care and Society*. Worcester, MA.

Rosenzweig, S., Reibel, D. K., Greeson, J. M. *et al.* (2003) Mindfulness-based stress reduction lowers psychological distress in medical students. *Teaching and Learning in Medicine*, **15**, 88–92.

Rowan, J. (2005) *The Transpersonal: Spirituality in Psychotherapy and Counselling*. Hove: Routledge.

Rumi (1994) *Say I Am You: Poems of Rumi* (trans. John Moyne and C. Barks). Athens, GA: Maypop Books.

Russell, B. (1955) *The Conquest of Happiness*. London: Allen & Unwin.

Safran, J. (1989) Insight and action in psychotherapy. *Journal of Integrative and Eclectic Psychotherapy*, **8**, 233–9.

—— (ed.) (2003) *Psychoanalysis and Buddhism: An Unfolding Dialogue*. Boston, MA: Wisdom Publications.

Safran, J. and Segal, Z. (1990) *Interpersonal Process in Cognitive Therapy*. New York: Basic Books.

Salzberg, S. and Kabat-Zinn, J. (1997) Mindfulness as medicine. In *Healing Emotions: Conversations with the Dalai Lama on Mindfulness, Emotions and Health* (ed. D. Goleman), Boston, MA: Shambhala, pp. 107–44.

Schore, A. (1994) *Affect Regulation and the Origin of the Self: The Neurobiology of Emotional Development*. Hillsdale, NJ: Lawrence Erlbaum.

Schwartz, J., Stoessel, P., Baxter, L. *et al.* (1996) Systematic changes in cerebral glucose metabolic rate after successful behavior modification treatment of obsessive-compulsive disorder. *Archives of General Psychiatry*, **53**, 109–13.

Segal, Z., Williams, J. and Teasdale, J. (2002) *Mindfulness-Based Cognitive Therapy for Depression*. New York: Guilford.

Semple, R., Lee, J. and Miller, L. (2006) Mindfulness-based cognitive therapy for children. In *Mindfulness-Based Treatment Approaches* (ed. R. Baer), New York: Academic Press, pp. 143–66.

Sethi, S. and Bhargaa, S. (2003) Relationship of meditation and psychosis: case studies. *Australian and New Zealand Journal of Psychiatry*, **37**, 382.

Shapiro, D. (1992a) Adverse effects of meditation: a preliminary study of long-term meditators. *International Journal of Psychosomatics*, **39**, 62–6.

Shapiro, D. H. (1992b) A preliminary study of long-term meditators – goals, effects, religious orientation, cognitions. *Journal of Transpersonal Psychology*, **24**, 23–39.

Shapiro, S. (2001) Poetry, mindfulness and medicine. *Family Medicine*, **33**, 505–7.

Shapiro, S. and Schwarz, G. (1999) Intentional systemic mindfulness: an integrative model for self-regulation and health. *Advances in Mind–Body Medicine*, **15**, 128–34.

Shapiro, S. L., Carlson, L. E., Astin, J. A. *et al.* (2006) Mechanisms of mindfulness. *Journal of Clinical Psychology*, **62**, 373–86.

Shapiro, S. L., Schwartz, G. E. and Bonner, G. (1998) Effects of mindfulness-based stress reduction on medical and premedical students. *Journal of Behavioral Medicine*, **21**, 581–99.

Shaw, R. (2004) The embodied psychotherapist: an exploration of the therapist's somatic phenomena within the therapeutic encounter. *Psychotherapy Research*, **14**, 271–88.

Silananda, U. (2002) *The Four Foundations of Mindfulness*. Boston, MA: Wisdom Publications.

Simmonds, J. (2004) Heart and spirit: research with psychoanalysis and psychoanalytic psychotherapists about spirituality. *International Journal of Psychoanalysis*, **85**, 951–72.

Singh, N., Wahler, A., Adkins, A. *et al.* (2003) Soles of the feet: a mindfulness-based self-control intervention for aggression by an individual with mild mental retardation and mental illness. *Research in Mental Disabilities*, **24**, 158–69.

Smith, A. (2006) 'Like waking up from a dream'. Mindfulness training for older people with anxiety and depression. In *Mindfulness-Based Treatment Approaches* (ed. R. Baer), New York: Academic Press, pp. 191–215.

Sole-Leris, A. (1992) *Tranquility and Insight*. Kandy: Buddhist Publication Society.

Speeth, K. (1982) On psychotherapeutic attention. *Journal of Transpersonal Psychology*, **14**, 141–60.

Stigsby, B., Rodenberg, J. and Moth, H. (1981) Electroencephalographic findings during mantra meditation (transcendental meditation). A controlled, quantitative study of experienced meditators. *Electroencephalography and Clinical Neurophysiology*, **51**, 434–42.

Strauss, A. and Corbin, J. (1990) *Basics of Qualitative Research: Grounded theory Procedures and Techniques.* Newbury Park, CA: Sage.

Suler, J. (1993) *Contemporary Psychoanalysis and Eastern Thought.* Albany, NY: State University of New York Press.

Symington, J. and Symington, N. (1996) *The Clinical Thinking of Wilfred Bion.* London: Routledge.

Teasdale, J. D. (1999) Emotional processing, three modes of mind and the prevention of relapse in depression. *Behaviour Research and Therapy,* **37**, S53–S77.

Teasdale, J. D., Moore, R. G., Hayhurst, H. *et al.* (2002) Metacognitive awareness and prevention of relapse in depression: empirical evidence. *Journal of Consulting and Clinical Psychology,* **70**, 275–87.

Telch, C., Agras, W. and Linehan, M. (2001) Treatment of binge eating with dialectical behaviour therapy. *Journal of Clinical and Consulting Psychology,* **6**, 1061–5.

Thera, N. (1965) *The Heart of Buddhist Meditation.* York Beach, ME: Weiser.

—— (1994) The power of mindfulness. In *The Vision of Dhamma* (2nd edn) (ed. N. Thera), Kandy: Buddhist Publication Society, pp. 69–116.

Thera, P. (1974) *The Buddha's Ancient Path.* Kandy: Buddhist Publication Society.

Urbanowski, F. and Miller, J. (1996) Trauma, psychotherapy and meditation. *Journal of Transpersonal Psychology,* **28**, 183–200.

Van der Kolk, B. (2002) Beyond the talking cure: somatic experience and subcortical imprints in the treatment of trauma. In *EMDR as an Integrative Psychotherapy Approach* (ed. F. Shapiro), Washington, DC: American Psychological Association, pp. 57–83.

VanderKooi, L. (1997) Buddhist teachers' experience with extreme mental states in western meditators. *Journal of Transpersonal Psychology,* **29**, 31–46.

VRI (1996) *Mahasatipatthana Sutta: The Great Discourse on the Establishing of Awareness.* Seattle, WA: Vipassana Research Institute.

Wallace, B. (2006) *The Attention Revolution: Unlocking the Power of the Focused Mind.* Boston, MA: Wisdom Publications.

Walshe, M. T. (1995) *The Long Discourses of the Buddha: A Translation of the Digha Nikaya.* Boston, MA: Wisdom Publications.

Weiss, M., Norlie, J. and Siegel, E. (2005) Mindfulness-based stress reduction as an adjunct to outpatient psychotherapy. *Psychotherapy and Psychosomatics,* **74**, 108–12.

Welch, S., Rizvi, S. and Dimidjian, S. (2006) Mindfulness in dialectical behavior therapy (DBT) for borderline personality disorder. In *Mindfulness-Based Treatment Approaches: Clinician's Guide to Evidence Base and Applications* (ed. R. Baer), Burlington, MA: Academic Press, pp. 117–42.

Wellings, N. and McCormick, E. (2006) *Nothing to Lose: Psychotherapy, Buddhism and Living Life*. London: Continuum.

Welwood, J. (2000) Reflection and presence: the dialectic of self-knowledge. In *Toward a Psychology of Awakening*, Boston: Shambhala, pp. 98–129 (also in *Journal of Transpersonal Psychology* (1997), **28**, 107–28).

Whyte, D. (1990) *Where Many Rivers Meet*. Langley, WA: Many Rivers Press.

Williams, J. and Swales, M. (2004) The use of mindfulness-based approaches for suicidal patients. *Archives of Suicide Research*, **8**, 315–29.

Williams, J. M. G., Teasdale, J. D., Segal, Z. V. *et al.* (2000) Mindfulness-based cognitive therapy reduces overgeneral autobiographical memory in formerly depressed patients. *Journal of Abnormal Psychology*, **109**, 150–5.

Witkiewitz, K., Marlatt, G. A. and Walker, D. (2005) Mindfulness-based relapse prevention for alcohol substance use disorders. *Journal of Cognitive Psychotherapy*, **19**, 211–28.

Wolfsdorf, B. A. and Zlotnick, C. (2001) Affect management in group therapy for women with posttraumatic stress disorder and histories of childhood sexual abuse. *Journal of Clinical Psychology/In Session*, **57**, 169–81.

Yorston, G. (2001) Mania precipitated by meditation: a case report and literature review. *Mental Health, Religion and Culture*, **4**, 209–13.

Index

mania 105
markers of mindfulness 37
Marlatt, G. 94, 95, 102
Martin, Jeffrey 77–9, 107
Maslow, Abraham 145–8, 156–7, 159, 164
Mathnawi (Rumi) 116–17
meaning, nodes of 44–5
medical students, mindfulness training for 130–6, 137
medical treatment, support for 59, 61
meditation 88–9; concentration meditation 27–8, 100–1, 154; electrophysiological research into 24–31, 50; forgiveness meditation 64, 72; and a fragile sense of self 153–4; insight meditation 6, 30, 114; Krishnamurti on 124; loving kindness meditation 72, 103; mindfulness meditation 6, 22–3, 26–8, 32, 37–46, 155; movement meditation 60–1, 111; negative motivations for 150; phases of 113; projective testing of 46–50; relaxation meditation 27–8; sitting meditations 111; training in group interventions 72; training in mindfulness-based cognitive therapy 64; training in mindfulness-based stress reduction 59–60; transcendental meditation 25, 26, 28, 39–40; and truth 157–8; walking meditation 60–1; zazen 25–6
memory: autobiographical 91–2; suspension of 52–4
mental discipline 13
mental disorders 85–109, 128–30, 139; alleviation and prevention 1–2; anger problems 93; anxiety disorders 87–9, 109; and D cognition 147; depression 85–6, 89–93, 96, 104; emotional regulation problems 93; Engler on 153; identifying clinical needs 125–8; intrusions 86, 92–3, 96–8; problems of relating 86, 103, 109;

problems of self 86, 103–4; trauma 98–102, 109
mental functioning, Cloninger's hierarchy of 145
mental health 138–65; and able-mindedness 148–50, 160–1, 164; and adaptation 148–52, 159–61, 164; and being 156–62; Cloninger's model of 143–6; defining good/positive 149; Engler on 152–6; and flow 140–2; Maslow on 146–8, 156–7; and peak experiences 146, 147–8, 156–7; and self-knowledge 162–4; spectrum of 148–52; and well-being 142–3
Mental Health Foundation 149
mental proliferation (*sankhara*) 10, 11–12, 13
metacognition 44, 45, 145
metacognitive awareness 91–2, 123
metapsychology 54
mind: Buddhist concepts of the 76; contemplation of the 14; divided model of the 66–7, 68; emotional 66–7; free 124; Freudian model of the 66; objects of the (*dhamma*) 12, 14; Plato's model of the 66; reasonable 66; reversal of the conditioning of the 46–9; wise 66, 68
mindful activity 111
mindful therapy 51–84, 139; adverse effects of 105–6; brain therapy 79–80; cognitive-behavioural therapies 58, 62–71; future developments 79–83; group interventions 71–3; implications for psychotherapy 74–9; integrating mindfulness and psychotherapy 73–4; and mental disorder 85–109; mindfulness-based stress reduction 58–62; psychodynamic therapies 51–8, 73–83; therapeutic actions of 106–9
Mindfulness Attention and Awareness Scale (MAAS) 31–2, 34, 43